Raptors

OF THE
PACIFIC NORTHWEST

THOMAS BOSAKOWSKI
and
DWIGHT G. SMITH

Frank Amato
PORTLAND

ACKNOWLEDGMENTS

JERRY LIGUORI

THE AUTHORS WISH TO THANK TREVOR BECKER FOR PRODUCING THE range maps, which were made under our direction. We are greatly appreciative of the many slides and photographs that were contributed and wish to thank Jerry Liguori, Frank Schleicher, Gerrit Vyn, Jean-Luc Cartron, Brian K. Wheeler, Jan Landis, David H. Ellis, Brian Caven, Daniel E. Varland, Jane Foreman, Scott Angus, Jim Zipp, Kara Donahue, Patricia Gayle, Richard Angus, Dave Zamos, and Steve Cox. We also thank Dr. Daniel E. Varland for reviewing first drafts of the species accounts for Peregrine Falcon, Bald Eagle, Northern Goshawk, and Northern Spotted Owl.

Published in 2002 by Frank Amato Publications, Inc.
P.O. Box 82112, Portland, Oregon 97282
(503) 653-8108
www.amatobooks.com

Softbound ISBN: 1-57188-236-7   Softbound UPC: 0-66066-00490-1

Front Cover Photos
Mount Baker: Thomas Bosakowski
Sharp-shinned Hawk: Jerry Liguori
Bald Eagle: Jerry Liguori
Spotted Owl: Gerrit Vyn

Back Cover Photo:
Gerrit Vyn

Title Page Painting (Ferruginous Hawk): Mark McCoy
Contents Photo: Osprey by Tom Bosakowski

Book Design: Tony Amato

Printed in Hong Kong

1 3 5 7 9 10 8 6 4 2

CONTENTS

INTRODUCTION . . . 4
SPECIES ACCOUNTS . . . 14

What is a Raptor?

Raptors are the eagles, hawks, falcons, kites, vultures, and owls of the bird world. Over the centuries raptors have become both symbol and metaphor for beauty, courage, swiftness, and above all, ferocity. After all, it was the imperial eagle which symbolized the might of Roman legions and the eagle standard led Napoleon's army into battle. As an interesting footnote to history, the Athenians preferred the owl of Athena. For various countries, including our own, raptors have been displayed as an emblem of strength, freedom, and power.

Raptors are by definition rapacious (predatory) birds which survive by hunting and killing other animals, often other birds, but also mammals and a wide variety of vertebrate and invertebrate animals. They possess sharp, hooked beaks for killing and tearing flesh, and strong grasping feet with sharp talons for catching, holding, or killing prey. The word raptor is a nontaxonomic term, but does not include shrikes, ravens, and many other birds which can also be seen as predatory. In fact, old-world tradition narrowly applies the term raptor only to the diurnal birds of prey, the eagles, hawks, and falcons. But this is not the Old World and the Raptor Research Foundation considers the term raptors to include both diurnal and nocturnal birds of prey.

Taxonomically, raptors belong to two different bird orders. The diurnal birds of prey are placed in the Order Falconiformes which includes eagles, hawks, falcons, and kites, while the owls are all placed in the Order Strigiformes. Until very recently, vultures were also considered Falconiformes, but they have been placed under the order Ciconiformes (AOU Checklist 2000), which includes storks, herons, and ibises. The 35-plus raptor species that occur in the Pacific Northwest range in size from the Bald

Sagebrush-Juniper desert in northern Oregon for open country raptors like Swainson's Hawk.

Extensive lodgepole pine forest at Chasm Provincial Park in central British Columbia; habitat for forest-nesting raptors such as Northern Goshawks and Great Grey Owls.

Eagle, which may reach 7 feet in wingspan to the diminutive Flammulated Owl, which generally averages only 6 inches in height to 14 inches in wingspan.

Raptors in the Landscape

As a group, raptors are widespread in the varied landscapes of the Pacific Northwest. In fact, few landscapes are without one or more raptor species. Some raptors such as the Red-tailed hawk and Great Horned Owl occur in a wide variety of habitats while others such as the Flammulated Owl and Great Grey Owl are species that seem to be more restricted in habitat use. While certain raptors like the Golden Eagle and Northern Goshawk are more commonly found in wilderness landscapes, others, such as the Barn Owl, Great Horned Owl, and Western Screech-Owl are much more tolerant of the human-modified landscapes such as agricultural and even residential areas. A few species like the Peregrine Falcon and Red-tailed Hawk may, on occasion, even occupy city interiors, nesting on skyscrapers and other buildings and foraging for pigeons, starlings, and other prey of city landscapes. Wherever they occur, raptors are important ecological components within their landscapes. They typically occupy the upper trophic levels and several species represent the top order consumers of the habitats in which they occur.

The Value of Raptors

For wildlife enthusiasts, raptors are valuable for aesthetic reasons, simply because they are wild free-flying creatures of remarkable beauty, speed, and agility, with a multitude of intriguing calls, displays, and behaviors. Not only are raptors the highlight of many field trips, but often they are the sole purpose of the expedition. For example, autumn hawk migration look-outs and winter feeding concentrations of Bald Eagles are sites that attract thousands of visitors each year. For others, however, the worth of a raptor must be more closely documented.

Ecologically, raptors function as important predators that help keep prey populations in check. Raptors are especially valuable in agricultural habitats because of their fondness for small mammals such as mice, rats, and rabbits. They help dampen outbreaks of these and other pests which may destroy crops and

Coastline is an important habitat for migrating and nesting hawks and falcons (Copalis, Washington).

transmit disease if left unchecked. Because they are top-level consumers, raptor populations have also served as a barometer of sorts for the environment. That is, any environmental perturbation such as pollution, habitat loss, or habitat alteration will often first be detected by changes in the highly-visible raptor populations. To illustrate, the impact of chlorinated hydrocarbons such as DDT and DDE were first noticed when reproduction of Osprey, Peregrine Falcon, and Bald Eagle populations declined precipitously. Scientists traced the decline to eggshell thinning which in turn was directly linked to pesticide contamination of the environment in attempt to control insects. In the forests, another species of raptor signaled another environmental crisis.

Declining numbers of Spotted Owls alerted the public to the rapidly disappearing old-growth forests which have recently been reduced to 5 to 10% of their original acreage in the Pacific Northwest (Bolsinger and Waddell 1993). In response, the President's Forest Plan was instituted to protect old-growth habitat for the threatened Spotted

Owl and many other imperiled species, including salmon and steelhead, which also depend on this valuable ecosystem.

Field Research on Raptors

Population Surveys are aimed at assessing the abundance and distribution of raptors in the landscape. The level of intensity can vary from simple roadside counts ("point counts"), roost counts, or migration counts to complete systematic surveys of nest sites within a designated area, which can provide valuable information on nesting densities. Demographic studies may also be involved whereby raptors are banded and/or color-marked to provide detailed data on nest site fidelity, mate fidelity, survival, and emigration – immigration dynamics within the population.

Nesting Ecology studies can include an analysis of territories and home ranges, often facilitated by the use of radiotelemetry. Researchers track radiotagged raptors, and data is often collected on habitat use within the home range. Most nest surveys also include a detailed analysis of habitat variables

Giant cliffs provide nest sites for raptors along the Fraser River in central British Columbia.

TOM BOSAKOWSKI

within a fixed distance of nest sites. In addition, field biologists may collect information on nest dimensions and construction. Probably the most important aspect of nesting ecology is analyzing the reproductive success of nesting pairs. Visits to active nests are made periodically throughout the nesting season to determine such parameters as clutch size, egg dates, brood size, productivity, development of young, and evidence of predation and disease on young.

Feeding Ecology studies are conducted to determine the food habits of raptors during a specified time period such as the nesting season, winter, or year-round. Food habits are determined by analysis of pellets and prey remains left around nest sites, roost sites, or plucking posts. Blind observations of adult raptors can be performed to directly observe prey items that are carried back to the nest, but such studies are generally too labor intensive since only a few items may be captured each day. Other feeding studies may examine hunting success rates or prey availability in the study area.

Wintering Ecology studies may include analysis of winter home ranges, winter feeding territories, habitat use, and roost site use and characteristics. Data is collected by direct observation with binoculars and spotting scopes, but radiotelemetry may be required for forest-dwelling raptors, or species with long-distance movements and large winter home ranges. Wintering studies are less frequently conducted than nesting studies, but could be instrumental in determining limiting factors for raptors that are permanent residents of the Northwest.

Banding Studies can provide valuable information on survival rates, longevity, site fidelity, dispersal, migration distance, and morphometrics for use in taxonomic studies. Raptors are usually banded at nest sites as advanced fledglings and adults may also be captured while defending their nest or attacking a baited trap containing live prey. In fall, hundreds of raptors are trapped and banded along migratory routes where raptors can concentrate in large numbers. Still, in winter, "roadside trappers" also capture and band raptors

7

High-elevation coniferous forests of the Canadian Rockies in eastern British Columbia can harbor species such as the Boreal Owl.

along country roads throughout their area. With the advent of solar-powered satellite transmitters, large raptors can be tracked over large migration distances for years and an accurate picture of individual migration routes can be obtained.

Management of raptors is often accomplished by protecting or manipulating their habitats. Habitat management can involve a variety of actions or activities to provide raptor populations with ample habitat for breeding, wintering, or migratory dispersal.

1. *Habitat Preservation* is accomplished by simply setting aside undisturbed land (preserves) with no active management other than to enforce specific land use restrictions on logging, mining, grazing, damming, road construction, development, and sometimes even recreation.

2. *Habitat Restoration/Improvement* is an active attempt to change the quality and characteristics of the habitat to provide improvements for the raptor(s) of concern and/or their prey. Restoration may include developing site-specific silvicultural (logging) prescriptions, prescribed burning, or other habitat mitigation actions such as creation of wetlands, ponds, or fields. In some cases, habitat may be plentiful, but nest sites may be limited. This situation is a prime example of where artificial nest sites (boxes and platforms) can be erected or snag creation (topping or killing live trees) can be accomplished to promote higher densities of snags for cavity-nesting raptors.

3. *Buffer Zones* are designed to provide protection around known nest sites and roost sites. Long-term buffers are designed to protect the habitat immediately surrounding the nest or roost (until several years after abandonment) from habitat alterations such as logging, construction, or development. Seasonal buffers are usually employed only during sensitive periods such as the nesting season or during fall salmon runs for Bald Eagles. Seasonal buffers are generally intended to reduce disturbance from human activities, but rarely do they protect the

habitat during the off-season. In order for the buffer system to function correctly, intensive annual population surveys using standardized protocols are necessary to insure that all nesting pairs or nest sites are found so that they can receive protective buffers. Another drawback is that the buffer radius is often driven by politics, rather than biology, and thus, the buffer is often too small to provide adequate protection for most individual pairs (Crocker-Bedford 1990).

4. *Powerline Safety Modifications* are an important and ongoing task to protect all kinds of raptors from electrocution (Olendorff et al. 1981). In open, arid, tree-less country, raptors are often tempted to perch on power poles and utility towers, and therefore these structures must be made to be safe for use by raptors. This can be done by modifying the position of arms, wires, and transformers.

In addition to habitat management, captive breeding, hacking, and egg/young

manipulations are sometimes performed in critically-endangered species to artificially induce a greater reproductive output within the population. In some cases, supplementation of food has been attempted to improve winter survival or nesting success of wild pairs. For example, carcasses of deer and rabbit (carrion) have been offered to some raptors such as eagles and stocking of trout in reservoirs has been attempted to entice nesting by Osprey.

Purpose and Scope of this Book

The purpose of this book is to inform natural-ists, birders, biologists, students, and teachers on the range, status, habits, ecology, and con-servation of raptors from the Pacific Northwest region. In addition, this book is also intended to function as a fully-referenced handbook for wildlife professionals, touching most of the important topics in life history, ecology, and conservation. The scope of this book is to provide timely, up-to-date infor-mation on raptors in Oregon, Washington, and British Columbia (hereafter called the Pacific Northwest). For each species account, we

View from a Golden Eagle nest ledge near Yakima Canyon, Washington.

attempted to include the most local and regional research information. However, when there was little known information available from the region, we tried to incorporate research from other western states and provinces. In a few cases, research was mentioned from eastern North America, but we avoided citing any literature from other continents. In cases where a long list of references was apparent, we often substituted a review article (e.g., Zarn 1974; Marshall 1992a, b; Sharp 1992), the *Birds of North America Series*, or books that reviewed a large number of research reports and studies (e.g., Stalmaster 1987; Johnsgard 1988, 1990; Palmer 1988). In this way, the reader can still trace back to the original research studies by reading the review article or book that is cited. Therefore, citation of a review article does not necessarily imply that the cited author did the original research or is the authoritative reference on the subject. Please be aware when a review article/book is substituted for a long list of original research.

Organization of this Book

This book is organized into 35 species accounts, each containing a range map, informative text, and a series of color photos. The text for each species is divided into subheadings for easy reference to important topics as follows:

• **Range.** In addition to range maps, we briefly describe distribution in the Pacific Northwest region, along with factors affecting range such as migratory status or elevation limits.

• **Status.** A brief summary of federal, state, and provincial listing status as well as evidence for declines, increases, range expansion, range contraction, and a brief listing of factors potentially affecting populations.

• **Habitat Requirements.** A review of habitat conditions required by the species during breeding, wintering, and/or migrating seasons.

Raptor watching in the beautiful Pacific Northwest (View of Mount Shuksan above Picture Lake in the Mount Baker Wilderness in the North Cascades of Washington).

• **Nesting.** Specific details for nests, their location, and associated habitat conditions such as stand characteristics, topography, and nest tree dimensions.

• **Eggs and Young.** Descriptions of eggs, egg dates, clutch size, and brood size or productivity are presented for most species where data exists for the region.

• **Roosting.** For a limited number of species, we list information about the numbers of birds attending roosts as well as characteristics of roost sites and surrounding habitats.

• **Hunting Behavior and Diet.** A brief description of hunting modes and techniques used along with a summary of major prey items taken in the region.

• **Territory and Density.** – Pertinent details about territory size, defense, and density of nesting pairs.

• **Surveys.** A review of special and general survey techniques which have been used to locate raptors and their nest sites and roost sites.

• **Conservation and Management.** A review of previous management techniques and plans which have been used or recommended, as well as suggestions by the authors when little has been done previously.

At the end of the book, three useful Appendices are presented which provide metric-English conversions (Appendix A), a glossary of ecological and ornithological terms (Appendix B), and a table summarizing general habitat use of raptors in the Pacific Northwest (Appendix C).

Photographs

Photographs are provided as an aid in the field identification of raptors and for the visual enjoyment and curiosity of readers as well. For a limited number of species, we also provide views of nest sites and habitats. Unless

The coniferous forests surrounding Mount Hood in Oregon provide habitat for Northern Goshawk and Sharp-shinned Hawk.

View of Mount Baker, Washington: raptors can be found from sea level to above timberline in the Pacific Northwest.

otherwise stated, photographs represent birds of unknown sex. In addition to photos, we also include length and wingspan measurements provided in Robbins et al. (1983) to assist with field identification. Because of the large number of popular field guides that are currently available with paintings, photographs, and descriptions of raptors, we do not provide detailed written descriptions of bird morphology, plumages, and field identification in this book. For more detailed descriptions and measurements of North American raptors, consult Wheeler and Clark (1995) and Johnsgard (1988, 1990).

Range Maps

The range maps presented in this book are taken primarily as tracings from the *Birds of North America* series, but a few were taken or modified from Johnsgard (1988, 1990), Campbell et al. (1990), and papers in the Western Raptor Management Symposium and Workshop sponsored by the National Wildlife Federation and published in 1989. The maps in this book should not be considered as authoritative boundaries, but rather as a general guide for assistance in raptor identification and understanding the general distribution patterns of raptors in the Pacific Northwest. On the maps, light green equals wintering range, dark green equals resident range, yellow equals breeding range, blue represents saltwater, and tan represents land where no ranges occur.

Listing Status

The legal status of raptors has been determined by federal, state, and provincial listing processes which are under periodic review and reconsideration as new data are collected on each species of concern. The federal government of the United States lists species as endangered, threatened, or species of concern. Under the Endangered Species Act of 1973, an endangered species is defined as "any species which is in danger of extinction throughout all or a significant portion of its range other than a species of the Class Insecta determined by the Secretary to constitute a pest whose protection under the provisions of this Act would present an overwhelming and overriding risk to man." A threatened species is defined as "any species which is likely to become an endangered species within the foreseeable future throughout all or a significant portion of its range."

Washington and Oregon list species as endangered, threatened, or sensitive, and candidates are species under examination for possible listing. These classifications are defined below.

• *Endangered:* any native species that is seriously threatened with extinction throughout all or a significant portion of its range.

• *Threatened:* any native species that is likely to become an endangered species within the foreseeable future throughout all or a significant portion of its range.

• *Sensitive:* any native species that is vulnerable or declining and is likely to become an endangered or threatened species throughout a significant portion of its range without cooperative management or removal of threats.

• *State Candidate:* any native species that is under review for possible listing as endangered, threatened, or sensitive. A species will be considered for designation as a state candidate if sufficient evidence suggests that its status may meet the listing criteria defined for endangered, threatened, or sensitive.

In British Columbia, provincial vertebrate animal tracking lists designate raptors as Red-Listed, Blue-Listed, or Yellow-Listed.

• *Red-Listed*: any indigenous species or subspecies considered to be extirpated, endangered, or threatened, such that Extirpated taxa no longer occur in British Columbia, but do occur elsewhere, Endangered taxa are facing imminent extirpation or extinction, and Threatened taxa are likely to become endangered if limiting factors are not reversed.

• *Blue-Listed :* any indigenous species or subspecies considered to be vulnerable and at risk, but not extirpated, endangered, or threatened. These species are of special concern because of characteristics that make them particularly sensitive to human activities or natural events.

• *Yellow-Listed:* any indigenous species or subspecies which is not at risk (secure) in the province. These species are managed at the habitat level by managing for a diversity of habitats in the province. In addition, some Yellow-Listed species are tracked which are vulnerable during times of seasonal concentration.

Units of Measurement

In the text we generally present the English system of measurement followed by the Metric System. Appendix A presents a handy table to use for easy conversion from one system to the other as well as the meaning of abbreviations.

References

At the end of the book, a complete list of references has been compiled from journal articles, symposium papers, government reports, and books that were cited in the species accounts. In most cases, we avoided citing unpublished reports unless readily available by writing to the issuing agency. In a few cases, where we could find no pertinent references, we cited our own initials (TB and DGS) to indicate unpublished field observations. For well-studied topics, we did not always attempt to list every known publication on the subject and often we used a review article to prevent extensive listing of references. In these cases, we apologize for not including some valuable and otherwise notable references.

TURKEY VULTURE (*Cathartes aura*)

Length 25"; Wingspan 72"

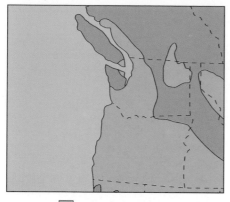

Breeding Range

Turkey Vulture.

GERRIT VYN

Range. In Washington, Smith et al. (1997) noted that it is most common in the lower forests of the eastern Cascades, uncommon and local in forests east of the Okanogan River and south to Rock Lake, and apparently absent from the Blue Mountains, Olympic Mountains and outer coast, which echoes the statement by Jewett et al. (1953) that the Turkey Vulture is far more common in eastern as opposed to western Washington. In northeastern Oregon, they are rare summer residents (Gilligan et al. 1994). In British Columbia, breeding is limited mostly to the southern parts of the province including Okanagan Valley and coastally from Quadra Island south to the southern tip of Vancouver Island (Campbell et al. 1990). Elevation of breeding sites ranged from near sea level to 3,180 feet (970 m). In winter it is rare to casual in parts of the interior of the Pacific Northwest. In autumn, large migrating flocks numbering hundreds of birds are annually recorded in the Gulf Islands of the Strait of Georgia and across southern Vancouver Island (Campbell et al. 1990). Large concentrations of over 200 vultures have been seen during migration at Malheur NWR in southeastern Oregon (Littlefield 1990).

Status. Although widespread and locally common throughout its range, suspected declines in populations resulted in the Turkey Vulture being Blue-Listed in 1972 and 1981, listed as a Species of Special Concern in 1982, and Local Concern in 1986 (Tate and Tate 1982; Ehrlich et al. 1988). Eggshell thinning was cited as the problem, but with the banning of DDT in 1972, the population seems to be making a recovery and expanding. Kirk and Mossman (1998) recently summarized population trends of Turkey Vultures in North America and noted that western and north-western populations increased based on BBS counts (Downes and Collins 1996).

Habitat Requirements. This scavenger is a widespread breeding species in open habitats or forested areas with frequent openings. Its preferred habitats are pastured rangeland, low-intensity agricultural areas, and wild areas with cliffs and rocky outcrops for nesting (Kirk and Mossman 1998). In the Pacific Northwest, it is found in farmlands, bluffs, pastures, fields, river mouths, and coastal areas including bays, inlets, and river mouths (Campbell et al. 1990). Smith et al. (1997) noted its absence in developed areas, as well as conifer forests at higher elevations throughout Washington.

Nesting. Turkey Vultures require small caves, cavities in cliffs, and cliff ledges, but occasionally they will nest in the tops of stumps or in large tree hollows with narrow, confining entrances. Isolation from human disturbance appears to be an important factor in nest-site selection (Kirk and Mossman 1998). Eight nests found in British Columbia were located in caves, crevices in cliffs, in boulder jumbles at the base of cliffs, and in mixed conifer and hardwood forests (Campbell et al. 1990). Nest substrates may consist of pebbles, leaves, and woody debris. Campbell et al. (1990) noted that one nest they recorded contained green Douglas-fir limbs, the other included large sticks and other woody debris. Nest height in cliffs ranged from 15 to 112 feet (4.6 to 34 m) above the base of the cliff (Campbell et al. 1990).

Eggs and Young. The eggs are white, marked with brown, and average about 2.81 x 1.91 inches (71.3 x 48.5 mm) in size (Herron et al. 1985). Normal clutch size of Turkey Vultures ranges from 1 to 3 eggs (avg. 2) and Jewett et al. (1953) recorded an early egg date in Washington as May 10. Egg dates for British Columbia clutches ranged from 1 May to 1 June, suggesting that eggs were laid in mid-April (Campbell et al. 1990). In British Columbia, brood size from 6 broods ranged from 1 to 2 young and dates of young in the nest ranged from mid-May to 23 August, suggesting a nesting period of 56 to 88 days (Ritter 1983; Campbell et al. 1990).

Hunting Behavior and Diet. These scavengers are opportunistic on wild and domestic carrion, but live prey are taken, albeit rarely. Most food consists of animals ranging in size from dead domestic livestock such as cows and sheep to wild ungulates down to rodents, shrews, chickens, other avian road kills, and herptiles including turtles, lizards, snakes, and frogs. Shellfish, insects and other invertebrates are also consumed when available (Kirk and Mossman 1998). Occasionally the Turkey Vulture kills and eats live food such as blackbirds at winter roosts (James and Neal 1986), fish from shallow waters (Jackson et al. 1978), captive animals (Smith 1982), or grasshoppers (Jewett et al. 1953). Turkey Vultures spend most of the day in soaring flight searching for food. Food is located with their keen eyesight and also by their excellent sense of smell (Kirk and Mossman 1998).

Roosting. Migrant and wintering concentrations may roost communally in trees or among cliffs, precipitous boulder shelves, and rocky debris (talus slopes). Roost sites may be ephemeral or permanent (used every day of the year – sometimes for decades) (Kirk and Mossman 1998).

A soaring Turkey Vulture displays an impressive wingspan.

Territory and Density. Turkey Vultures do not appear to be very territorial as nests are often found in close proximity. Densities in the Pacific Northwest reflect abundance of food, roost sites, and nest sites. Adults arrive on territories in interior British Columbia between late March and mid-May (Cannings et al. 1987). Smith et al. (1997) noted that their comparative rarity in northeastern Washington probably reflected the lack of cliffs and other suitable nest sites. Turkey Vulture pairs can nest as close as 305 to 512 feet (93 to156 m) apart (Coleman and Fraser 1989).

Surveys. Population counts of the Turkey Vulture are facilitated by its soaring flight which makes it highly visible and its habit of roosting and nesting communally. Counts at roost sites can provide reasonably accurate information on local populations, provided all local roost sites can be found. Observing flight direction of birds in evening hours and in early morning hours can generally facilitate locating roost sites.

Conservation and Management. As a scavenger feeding on road kills and other carrion, the Turkey Vulture is generally acknowledged to be a beneficial bird that deserves the protection afforded it by many states. Important causes of mortality include predation on eggs and young, and occasionally roosting adults by mammal predators (Kirk and Mossman 1998), owl predation, starvation, being killed by vehicles while feeding on road kills, electrocution from power lines, chemical contamination, shooting, and occasionally trapping. Jewett et al. (1953) noted that Turkey Vultures in Washington were sometimes caught in predatory animal traps baited with scent. Conservation measures designed to protect and increase the Turkey Vulture population have focused on providing for its protection and the use of organic farming which dramatically reduces the hazards of Turkey Vultures being poisoned by contaminants. Some suggested farming practices include the use of organic farming, use of smaller fields, promotion of farming practices that use a mix of agriculture fields, pastures, and nearby woodlots for nesting and roosting (Kirk and Mossman 1998).

Turkey Vulture feeds on a roadkill.

OSPREY (*Pandion haliaetus*)

Length 22"; Wingspan 54"

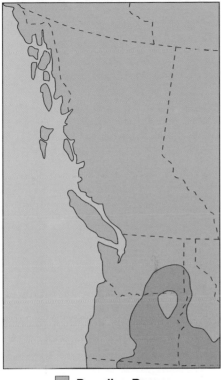

Breeding Range

Osprey.

Range. In Oregon, the Osprey ranges predominantly throughout the western half of the state from the Cascades west, although some nesting occurs scattered throughout the Blue Mountains (Csuti et al. 1997). In Washington, its breeding distribution extends over much of the state except perhaps in the southeastern lowlands and deserts (Henny and Anthony 1989). Distribution west of the Cascades is from Bellingham to the Columbia River. In British Columbia, the entire province is considered breeding range (Godfrey 1986) and nesting occurs from sea level up to about 3,350 feet (1,070 m) in elevation (Campbell et al. 1990). The species is highly migratory in the Pacific Northwest, migrating in September to Mexico and South America for winter and returning in April and May to breed (Zarn

1974; Henny and Anthony 1989). The earliest spring record for Malheur NWR in southeastern Oregon is 15 March (Littlefield 1990).

Status. Osprey populations declined sharply over much of the Pacific Northwest in the 50s and 60s, but have steadily increased since that time to a nearly complete recovery. Concern for this species arose after numbers plummeted after World War II after the introduction of DDT as a pesticide (Newton 1979). However, since the federal ban on DDT in 1972, population numbers have increased in eastern populations where more complete population monitoring has been recorded (Spitzer et al. 1978). Apparently, the problem was less severe in the western United States where few populations had been extirpated (Henny and Anthony 1989). Osprey populations probably declined largely as a result of pesticide contamination, the removal of nesting trees, degradation of river and lake environmental quality, boating and other human disturbances on nesting lakes, and shooting (Henny et al. 1978). Surveys in Washington estimate up to 260 to 290 nesting pairs in the state (Henny and

Anthony 1989). A similar trend is also apparent in Oregon from 1976 to 1993 after the ban on DDT in 1973 (Henny and Kaiser 1996). Osprey populations have noticeably increased in California over the last decade due, at least in part, to decreased pesticide residues in the environment (California Department of Fish and Game 1992). The Osprey has no special status in the Pacific Northwest, but was listed as a "state monitor" species in Washington (Rodrick and Milner 1991). Breeding Bird Survey routes on Pacific Northwest National Forests indicated a significant increase from 1968 to 1989, although statewide trends for Oregon and Washington were not significant from 1980 to 1989 (Sharp 1992).

Habitat Requirements. Foraging exclusively on fish, Ospreys typically nest in the vicinity of productive bodies of water, including large rivers, big lakes, estuaries, bays, and reservoirs (Kahl 1971; Johnson and Melquist 1973; Call 1978). The two basic habitat requirements for the Osprey are: 1) availability of large trees and/or snags for nest building and perches, and 2)

Osprey powerstroke.

productive water source providing abundant food (Kahl 1971; Johnson and Melquist 1973).

Nesting. Ospreys usually nest in fairly open situations along shorelines where forest cover is variable, and may or may not be present. Nest sites can also be well hidden in mature forest habitat, but can also occur in open country such as deserts, grasslands, agricultural land, and tidal flats. Their large stick nest is typically constructed on the top of tall, broken-top trees, snags, utility poles, buildings, pilings, silos, and high-tension towers (Call 1978; Henny and Kaiser 1996). In British Columbia, most tree nests (56% of 395 nests) were in dead trees, including black cottonwood and 5 species of conifers, whereas nests on man-made structures (44%) included wood pilings (53%), cross members of wooden power poles (32%), navigation lights/buoys (8%), and other structures (Campbell et al. 1990). Ospreys prefer to have accessory perches available for sunning and roosting near the nest tree (Zarn 1974; Call 1978). Sites that offer accessory perches within view of the nest are preferred (Zarn 1974). The majority of Osprey nests were less than a mile to the closest river (Henny and Kaiser 1996). However, nests have been known to occur up to 6 miles from fishing grounds (Sharp 1992).

Osprey in flight.

Osprey nest on farm tower in northern Washington.

Osprey nest on top of telephone pole along the Deschutes River, Oregon.

Osprey nest on top of white spruce near Horsefly, British Columbia.

Osprey nest on a snag in a marsh, Montesano, Washington.

Osprey nest on pilings in the Columbia River, Washington side.

Osprey nest on a powerline tower in Idaho.

Eggs and Young. The eggs are white or pinkish white in color, blotched with reddish brown and are 2.4 x 1.8 inches (61 x 45.7 mm) in size (Herron et al. 1985). In British Columbia, clutch size for 39 clutches ranged from 2 to 4 eggs with 54% having 3 eggs and brood size for 412 broods ranged from 1 to 4 birds with 54% having 2 young (Campbell et al. 1990).

Hunting Behavior and Diet. The diet of Ospreys is almost exclusively fish, although carrion and small mammals are occasionally eaten (Sharp 1992). Hunting is generally performed by soaring and circling over open water until a fish is spotted, or less often by scanning from a high perch along the edge of a body of water. When prey is spotted, the Osprey tucks its wings, dives, and then pushes its talons forward just before hitting the water, and sometimes it completely submerges for a second or two before rising heavily with a fish in its talons.

Territory and Density. Ospreys do not typically defend a definable territory, but will defend the area immediately around the nest (Johnsgard 1990). Around lakes, nests were spaced about 1,300 feet (398 m) apart, and about 5,360 feet (1,637 m) apart in forests, but Ospreys may nest semi-colonially where their population is dense in areas of high fish abundance (Sharp 1992). In British Columbia, the densest population is in the vicinity of Creston and Nelson where some 140 pairs nest (Campbell et al. 1990). Some Ospreys may forage up to 5 to 6 miles (8 to 10 km) from their nest (Sharp 1992).

Surveys. Light aircraft or helicopters or boats are usually used to survey the shorelines of lakes, reservoirs, and rivers, while observers closely watch the tops of all snags and broken-off trees for the presence of nests (Call 1978). Roadside surveys or hiking along rivers and shorelines could also be used to augment aerial and boat survey efforts. Observers should make periodic roadside stops (quarter-mile) and scan the sky over the shoreline for soaring/flying Ospreys for 5-minute periods. Since we found that Ospreys respond readily to whistled imitations of their calls, we suggest that tape-recorded broadcasts of Osprey calls could also be played to increase detection rates in heavily forested areas. Stations should be sampled in a "leap-frog" pattern to decrease spatiotemporal bias.

Conservation and Management. In areas lacking potential nest sites, erection of artificial platforms has been an effective management tool for encouraging nesting by Ospreys (Houston and Scott 1992). Along the Umpqua River in Oregon, live trees were topped and a flat 2x4-foot square platform was fixed on top to encourage nest building, which eventually resulted in a 54% platform occupancy by Ospreys (Witt 1990). On the Willamette River in Oregon, Ospreys have shown an apparent learned response to nesting on utility structures, such that nest sites are almost unlimited in that area now (Henny and Kaiser 1996). In remote areas, it is recommended that camp

Osprey.

Osprey perched on telephone pole.

• No timber or snags to be cut within 200 feet (61 m) of known Osprey breeding waters (except clearing danger trees for roads and campgrounds).
• Beyond the 200-foot (61 m) buffer, an additional one-fourth-mile buffer should be set aside where a minimum of two dominant live trees and two desirable snags per acre are retained.
• Beyond the one-fourth-mile buffer, all suitable "broken tops", snags or live trees should be left standing for a distance of two miles.
• Within 660 feet (200 m) of nests, 3 to 5 potential nest/roost trees should be left. Potential nest trees are either live or dead (snags) with broken-off tops. They must be tall enough to permit an unrestricted view (often of fishing grounds), generally well above the canopy (Johnson and Melquist 1973).
• Close management season within 660 feet (200 m) of nests during the period from April 1 to August 15.

sites should not be located within 0.7 mile (1 km) of occupied nests, and hiking trails should not come within 300 feet (91 m) of the nest (Rodrick and Milner 1991). Kahl (1971) described a habitat management plan for the Osprey on Lassen National Forest in California as summarized below:

Close-up of Osprey nest structure built on top of a white spruce tree.

WHITE-TAILED KITE (*Elanus leucurus*)
Length 14.5"; Wingspan 40"

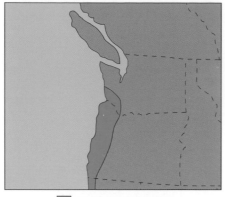

Resident Range

White-tailed Kite hunting from a low shrub.

Range. The range of the White-tailed Kite extends from the southwestern Washington lowlands, the Oregon Coast Range and Willamette Valley, south into California. In the southwestern lowlands of Washington there are some recent records of these kites in Pacific, Wahkiakum, and Lewis Counties which are currently expanding their range northward (Smith et al. 1997). Recent nestings have been documented in the Willamette Valley near Medford and Corvallis (Csuti et al. 1999). In southeastern Oregon, nesting has been documented for Malheur NWR (Littlefield 1990).

Status. This elegant raptor has no federal or state status, but population declines have been noted nationwide during the 1980s and 1990s (Dunk 1995). However, Martin (1989) reports populations in Oregon and California are increasing possibly because nomadic responses to variable prey densities can result in periodic fluctuations and irregular occurrence within a given population.

Habitat Requirements. Nesting habitat occurs in wooded riparian habitats in close proximity to open hunting habitats such as commercial farmlands, open grasslands, meadows, emergent wetlands, and lightly wooded areas (Martin 1989). Specific associations with plant species for foraging or nesting are not apparent, although vegetation structure and prey base may be significant factors in nest-site selection (Dunk 1995). Lightly grazed or ungrazed fields provide the best foraging habitat and most nests are placed near forest/grass edges (Dunk 1995).

Nesting. The nests usually occur in the upper one third of the nest tree which can be variable in height. Nest trees may range from 10 to 170 feet tall (3-52 m) and can occur as single, isolated trees or in large stands at least 250 acres (100 ha) (Dunk 1995). In the Sacramento Valley, 8 of 22 nests were placed in treetops, within the top three feet of the canopy (Erichsen et al. 1996).

Eggs and Young. Eggs average 1.7 x 1.3 inches (42.5 x 32.8 mm) in size (Bent 1937). Clutch size is large, ranging from 3 to 6 eggs (avg. 4.12) and average fledged brood size is 3.2 young (Johnsgard 1990). At least 46% of nest failures in the

Adult White-tailed Kite in flight.

Sacramento Valley were attributed to displacement by the later-arriving Swainson's Hawk (Erichsen et al. 1996).

Roosting. During non-breeding times, the species can be quite gregarious, roosting in numbers up to 100 birds (Small 1974). Roosts are established in trees or tall shrubs (Dunk 1995). Roosts may be sensitive to human disturbance, one roost in California was abandoned the day after it was repeatedly disrupted by all-terrain vehicles (Dunk 1995).

Hunting Behavior and Diet. White-tailed Kites feed primarily on small rodents (especially *Microtus spp.*), but also take other small mammals, lizards, snakes, birds, and insects (Bent 1937). Several authors have suggested that this species is an obligate Microtine (vole) predator (review by Martin 1989). They hunt almost exclusively by hovering above open ground (15-75 feet or 5-25 m) with subsequent diving upon prey, and perch hunting is rarely used (Dunk 1995).

Territory and Density. Territory size is small and averaged 178 acres (72 ha) in Long Beach, California (Waian 1973) and 109 acres (43.6 ha) in San Diego (Henry 1983). No data are available for Oregon or Washington.

Survey Methods. This open-country raptor is a good candidate for road transect surveys using either continuous low-speed driving (Craighead and Craighead 1956) or point-count observation stations at regular intervals (Kochert 1986). During road surveys, 68% of kites were in flight, and nearly half (34%) of these birds were hovering (Erichsen et al. 1996). If nesting data is desired, transects should be run during the breeding season and nest searches should be conducted in conjunction with sightings or displays that occur on survey routes (Erichsen et al. 1996). Broadcasts of conspecific calls (Kochert 1986) may be helpful in pinpointing the location of the nest in large stands that are difficult to walk through (i.e., heavy brush and thickets).

Conservation and Management. Riparian buffer strips or small deciduous woodlots probably serve as primary nesting and roosting sites in agricultural areas. This species probably does not occur in most National Forests or private commercially-harvested timberlands because of its preference for open grassland habitat. Martin (1989) suggested the following management recommendations for White-tailed Kites: 1) minimize chemical contamination of the environment (i.e., rodenticides, pesticides, herbicides, fertilizers), 2) protect wetlands and riparian habitats, 3) standardize census techniques and consider prey fluctuations, weather, land-use practices, and behavior when estimating Kite abundance.

The aerial White-tailed Kite most often seen flapping and hovering.

Bald Eagle (*Haliaeetus leucocephalus*)
Length 32"; Wingspan 80"

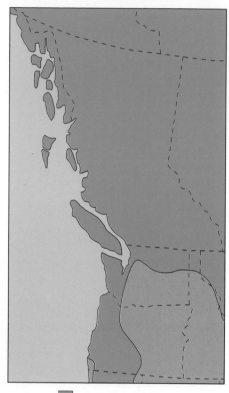

Resident Range

First-year adult Bald Eagle.

Range. In Oregon and Washington, the breeding range of the Bald Eagle occurs primarily in forested regions west of the Cascade crest that support salmon and steelhead runs, and in the northeastern mountains of Washington. Most nesting habitat in Washington is located in the San Juan Islands and on the Olympic Peninsula coastline (Grubb 1976), with other habitat along Hood Canal, on the Kitsap Peninsula, in Island County and southwestern Washington (U.S. Fish and Wildlife Service 1986). GAP Analysis for Washington also suggests that they are uncommon breeders along large interior lakes and reservoirs (Smith et al. 1997). Most Bald Eagles wintering in Washington are found along the Skagit, Nooksack, and Sauk River systems, in the Puget Trough, on the Olympic Peninsula, and in the Columbia Basin (U.S. Fish and Wildlife Service 1986). In British Columbia, the species is common on the coast, but locally and widely distributed in the interior (Godfrey 1986) with only local breeding in the northern half of the province (Campbell et al. 1990). Nesting occurs from sea level up to 4,500 feet (1,370 m) in elevation in British Columbia (Campbell et al. 1990). Most breeding Bald Eagles in Washington are believed to remain in the vicinity of their nests for the winter or move relatively short distances to lower elevations or to a food supply, and are joined by many that nest in Canada and Alaska (U.S. Fish and Wildlife Service 1986). Fall movements in British Columbia are protracted throughout the fall into early winter depending on salmon spawning and the number of spent carcasses (Campbell et al. 1990).

Status. When white settlers first arrived in Washington, there were an estimated 6,500 eagles in early summer populations. Early declines in Bald Eagle populations were attributed to human persecution and destruction of riparian, wetland, and coniferous forest habitats. Loss of water quality, contamination of estuaries, and commercial exploitation of salmon runs have reduced carrying capacity for eagles (Stinson et al. 2001). However, another important factor that contributed to declines of Bald Eagle populations was environmental contamination with DDE (dichloro-diphenyl-dichloroethyhlene), a metabolite of DDT (dichloro-diphenyl-trichloroethane) which worked its way into the aquatic food chain (Grier 1982). Various legal and management measures, including the banning of DDT in 1972 and development and implementation of the Pacific Bald Eagle Recovery Plan (U. S. Fish and Wildlife Service 1986) and local bald eagle management plans, have contributed to the continuing recovery of the Bald Eagle breeding population in Oregon and Washington, where it is still listed as threatened. The Bald Eagle is listed as a federally-threatened species in the US, but some talk about delisting is in progress. In British Columbia, this eagle did not decline

Juvenile Bald Eagle perched on telephone pole at Skagit Flats, Skagit, Washington.

Bald Eagle nest in dead topped tree with adjacent accessory perch tree (with adult) from Riffe Lake, Washington.

appreciably along the Pacific Coast (D. Hancock, pers. comm.) and has not received special status, remaining today on the provincial Yellow List.

Habitat Requirements. The Bald Eagle is usually found in close association with the shorelines of freshwater, estuarine, and marine ecosystems that provide abundant prey and suitable habitat for nesting and communal roosting (Stalmaster 1987). Preferred nesting habitat consists of multi-storied old-growth stands, or mature stands with residual old-growth components, dominated by conifers (Anthony et al. 1982; U.S. Fish and Wildlife Service 1986) in proximity to available food sources, primarily rivers or lakes with abundant populations of fish or waterfowl (Watson et al. 1991).

Nesting. Bald eagles typically select large nest trees, rarely less than 30 inches (76.2 cm) in diameter (Anthony et al. 1982), which are usually the tallest tree within the stand (Stalmaster 1987). A tall nest tree ensures an open flight path, an unobstructed view, and structure that is capable of supporting their massive nests. Nests are typically built near the top of one of the larger and more dominant trees available, and with a prominent topographic location and unobstructed view of the water (U.S. Fish and Wildlife Service 1986). Douglas-fir and Sitka spruce within 300 yards of open water are often used as nest trees, as are black cottonwood trees near rivers (Anderson et al. 1986). Other large trees near nest sites are needed for alternate nests and perches (U.S. Fish & Wildlife Service 1986). In British Columbia, 95% of 511 nests were in conifers (live or dead) along the coast, but most nests (67% of 73) in the interior were in deciduous trees (Campbell et al. 1990). Nest sites in Oregon were primarily (84%) within one mile of water (Anthony and Isaacs 1989). Nest sites in western Washington were located an average of 282 feet (86 m) from open water, ranging from 15 to 2,640 feet (5 to 800 m) (Grubb 1980). Nest sites in Barkley Sound, British Columbia, averaged only 138 feet (42 m) from high tide (Vermeer and Morgan 1989). Bald Eagles are sensitive to disturbance, and absence of human activities near nests increases reproductive success (U.S. Fish and Wildlife Service 1986), although pairs in urban or disturbed areas are often successful. Of 45 nests in western Washington, residential shoreline development was the greatest source of disturbance to nesting eagles, and nests averaged 735 feet (224 m) (Watson and Pierce 1998).

Eggs and Young. The eggs are white and average size is 2.8 x 2.1 inches (70.5 x 54.2 mm) (Bent 1937). Egg dates for 118 clutches

Adult Bald Eagle in flight at Skagit Flats, Skagit, Washington.

in British Columbia ranged from 12 February to 27 June and clutch size ranged from 1 to 3 eggs, with 63% having 2 eggs (Campbell et al. 1990). Brood size ranged from 1 to 3 young, with 60% having 1 young.

Roosting. Preferred communal winter roost sites occur in larger, older trees in uneven-aged conifers with old-growth components (Anthony et al. 1982) that provide thermal and wind protection (U.S. Fish and Wildlife Service 1986). On Washington's Nisqually River, 8 of 9 winter communal roosts were found in old-growth forest (Stalmaster and Kaiser 1997a). In Oregon, the average age of roost trees was found to be 236 years, ranging from 100 to 535 years of age (Keister and Anthony 1983). On the upper John Day River in Oregon, 66% of winter night roosts were in conifers, 33% were in black cottonwoods, and 2% were in mixed deciduous-juniper (Isaacs et al. 1996). Preferred roost sites are close to feeding areas, though they can be as far as 9 miles away (Keister and Anthony 1983), and low human disturbance is important for roosting and foraging in winter (Hansen et al. 1980; U.S. Fish and Wildlife Service 1986). On Washington's Nooksack River, winter populations of Bald Eagles peak in January with numbers reaching 100 eagles (Stalmaster et al. 1979) and a minimum of 127 to 200 eagles wintered in the upper Columbia River (Fielder and Starkey 1980). Large winter communal roosts have also been documented in the Klamath Basin of southern Oregon. Here, 5 communal roosts including Bear Valley, Mt. Dome, Three Sisters, Caldwell, and Cougar supported over 500 bald eagles in winter (Keister et al. 1987). These roosts were all in conifer stands at high elevations from 4,600 to 6,170 feet (400 to 1,880 m).

Hunting Behavior and Diet. Winter concentrations of Bald Eagles usually occur in areas of high availability of fish, waterfowl

First-year adult Bald Eagle.

(Keister et al. 1987; Frenzel and Anthony 1989), domestic sheep carcasses (Della Sala et al. 1989), snowshoe hares, and deer carcasses (Frenzel 1984). Along the Columbia River, eagles acquired food by hunting live prey (57%), scavenging (24%), and pirating (19%) (Watson et al. 1991). Here, the main prey group was fish (71%), but waterfowl and seabirds made-up the remainder of the diet. In three areas of western Washington, nesting bald eagle diets were comprised of 53% birds, 34% fish, 9% mammals, and 4% invertebrates (Knight et al. 1990). Bald Eagle nests are most often associated with aquatic foraging areas in Washington (Anthony et al. 1982). Perches used by foraging Bald Eagles are in tall trees located near feeding areas that give a good view of the surrounding area (U.S. Fish and Wildlife Service 1986). Various techniques are used by Bald Eagles to acquire fish or waterfowl, including swooping from flight, swooping from a perch, wading and capturing prey with the bill, and ice-fishing using the talons or bill to snag prey from open water (Johnsgard 1990).

Territory and Density. The nests are often regularly spaced along shorelines at intervals of 1 to 6 miles (1.6 to 10 km). For Bald Eagles in western Washington, the minimum nearest-neighbor nest distance between active nests was 1.0 mile (1.6 km) for the San Juan Islands, 1.7 miles (2.7 km) for the Olympic Peninsula, 2.4 miles (3.8 km) for Puget Sound, 1.5 miles (2.5 km) for Hood Canal, 4.9 miles (7.9 km) for Grays Harbor and south, and 4.0 miles (6.4 km) for inland lakes and rivers (Grubb 1980). This spatial distribution of nests does not necessarily imply an area of active defense against all other eagles (Grubb 1980). Linear nest density for Barkley Sound, British Columbia, averaged 0.07 per mile (1.1 nests per 10 km) of shoreline (Vermeer and Morgan 1989).

Survey Methods. The presence of large water bodies with active salmon and steelhead runs and nearby mature forest create potential habitat for nesting or roosting Bald Eagles. Surveys can be conducted along rivers and lake shorelines by hiking, driving (Stalmaster et al. 1979), boating (Ralph

1980, Stalmaster and Kaiser 1997a), or by flying in helicopters or fixed-wing aircraft (Call 1978; Grubb 1980; Anthony et al. 1999). See also Osprey. Aerial surveys should be flown on days with excellent visibility (no overcast) during mid-day so the search area has direct sunlight (no shadows). In most cases, it is desirable to make two passes in each drainage, with one pass on either side of the drainage. Boat surveys are an effective and cheaper option. To survey, the boat should travel at low speeds, about 100 to 200 feet (30 to 60 m) offshore while observers attempt to "skyline" the nest or perching adults, but several passes may be necessary to adequately survey the area (Call 1978). A study in Oregon (Anthony et al. 1999) reported that the precision of population estimates could be improved with the "double survey method" – using two different survey methods at the same time (e.g., boat and aerial or car and aerial).

Conservation and Management. Bald Eagles typically nest and roost in mature

Juvenile first-year Bald Eagle in flight.

trees or snags that are isolated from human disturbances. Snags and dead-topped live trees are important, providing perch and roost sites and should also be retained around eagle nests and roosts. The Forest Service proposed a 5-chain (100 meter) protection zone which was supported by disturbance data collected by Grubb (1980). To support eagle nesting densities in southeast Alaska, Gende et al. (1998) suggested that no-harvest buffer zones needed to be at least 300 meters. Stalmaster and Kaiser (1997b) found that ordnance explosions (blasting), low-level helicopter flights, and boating should be restricted near eagle foraging areas. Their findings suggest that the recommended buffers zones of 1,320 to 2,640 feet (400 to 800 m) (USFWS 1986) would be effective for boats and helicopters, but marginal for blasting.

In Washington, a cooperative Site Management Plan is developed whenever disrupting activities (logging, construction, blasting, mining) are proposed near a verified nest territory or communal roost (Rodrick and Milner 1991). Instead of applying a standard buffer width, Washington Department of Fish and Wildlife works with land-owners using a flexible, territory zoning concept to design site-specific management plans. Site plans have a permanently protected core around the nest tree or roost site and are surrounded by a seasonal buffer zone (1 January to 15 August for nests, 1 November to 1 April for winter roosts) known as the conditioned area, where some activities are permitted during the off season. Clearcutting is generally not allowed, but prescriptions for selective logging may be implemented (Rodrick and Milner 1991). Nearly two-thirds of nests occur on private land in Washington, so the future for Bald Eagles could once again be jeopardized without careful management and conservation of super dominant trees for nesting, perching, and roosting (Stinson et al. 2001).

NORTHERN HARRIER (*Circus cyaneus*)

Length 16.5"; Wingspan 42"

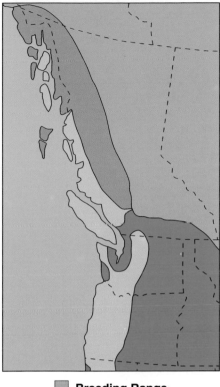

Adult male Northern Harrier.

Breeding Range

Resident Range

Wintering Range

Range. The Northern Harrier is a permanent resident in the Pacific Northwest. Washington records are concentrated in the arid, open lands of the southeast deserts and steppe country, but breeding is occassional throughout the Puget Trough, but less common along the southwestern coastal zone (Smith et al. 1997). In Oregon, it also breeds predominantly east of the Cascade Range in open, arid country, but also occurs widely throughout the Willamette Valley (Csuti et al. 1997). The harrier breeds locally throughout British Columbia, except for Queen Charlotte Island (Godfrey 1986).

Nesting occurs from sea level up to 3,300 feet (1,010 m) in elevation in British Columbia, and in the fall, many individuals migrate south from September to mid-October (Campbell et al. 1990).

Status. Despite their relative rarity and patchy distribution, Northern Harriers have not shown obvious signs of declining in the Pacific Northwest. As of 1987, the Northern Harrier was considered common in Oregon and Washington (Martin 1989). Significant declines were not observed on Breeding Bird Survey routes on National Forests of Oregon and Washington, although it is typically rare or absent because of the high elevation of many of these forests and the paucity of large open wetlands (Sharp 1992).

Habitat Requirements. The Northern Harrier is essentially an open-country species, usually nesting or hunting in low-lying wetland marshes, estuaries, bogs, fields, pastures, cropland, meadows, burns, and clearcuts (Johnsgard 1990). In these habitats, harriers use tall grasses and wetland forbs as cover for nesting and roosting. The species is more common in areas where suitable habitat remains free of disturbance, mainly from intensive agriculture and grazing.

Nesting. Harrier nests occur on the ground, hidden in tall grasses, sedges, reeds, rushes, cattails, willows, or shrubby vegetation (Brown and Amadon 1968; Johnsgard 1990). Nests are built in about 7 to 14 days and are made of grass, reeds, forbs, weeds, water-plants (MacWhirter and Bildstein 1996) and lined somewhat with feathers (Gabrielson and Jewett 1953). Either sex may select nests which are often surrounded by wet areas, although very few are reported from brackish or salt water (MacWhirter and Bildstein 1996). Both sexes carry nesting material to the site, but the male will transfer materials to the female with and aerial pass or simply by landing at the site (MacWhirter and Bildstein 1996). In British Columbia, most nests (64%, n=52) were discovered in wet or dry cattail and bulrush marshes, while other nests were located in emergent vegetation bordering lakes, beaver ponds, hardhack and spruce bogs, open burns, and open fields with shrub growth (Campbell et al. 1990).

Eggs and Young. The eggs are bluish-white, sometimes sparsely spotted or smeared with pale brown (Godfrey 1986) and average size in Alberta was 1.8 x 1.4 inches (45.6 x 36.2 mm) (Sealy 1967). In British Columbia, egg dates ranged from 18 April to 29 June, clutch

A juvenile Northern Harrier riding the wind with its wings held in a classic dihedral position.

size for 52 clutches ranged from 1 to 6 eggs, with 67% having 4 or 5 eggs, and brood size for 21 broods ranged from 2 to 6 young with 56% having 4 or 5 young (Campbell et al. 1990). Productivity at 11 nests in Alberta averaged 1.9 fledglings per nest attempt (Sealy 1967). In western Washington, the earliest clutch completion date is 12 April and the latest fledging date was 16 July (Thompson and McDermond 1985).

Roosting. During winter, harriers often aggregate into winter communal roosts, sometimes with more than a dozen birds in attendance (Bosakowski 1983; Christiansen and Reinert 1990). As with nest sites, harriers roost on the ground, hidden amongst tall reeds and grasses. The roost sites are often traditional, used over many years.

Hunting Behavior and Diet. Harriers feed mostly on voles and other small mammals, birds, frogs, reptiles, and insects that inhabit open habitats. The Northern Harrier usually hunts on the wing with low coursing flights over the ground, making quick plunges to grab prey. While gliding, the harrier will ride the wind like a kite with its wings held in a dihedral pattern (tilted upward) for maximum aerodynamic stability and rapid quartering. Sometimes, prey will be spotted briefly, and the harrier will respond by hovering in place to try and gain another glimpse of the prey's location. Harriers will

Adult female Northern Harrier in Richland, Washington area.

also hunt from a low perch (fence post, bush, or mound) or the ground while they are resting. In one study, harriers spent an average of 57% of their time perched on the ground (Craighead and Craighead 1956).

Territory and Density. Harriers are not strongly territorial during the breeding season, except near nests, but adult females may be territorial during winter (MacWhirter and Bildstein 1996). In Idaho, breeding home range was determined to be an average of about 4,000 acres (1,620 ha) for males and 2,800 acres (1,133 ha) for females (Martin 1987).

Survey Methods. During winter, periodic survey counts can be made to assess the population size of wintering harriers at communal roosts (Bosakowski 1983; Kochert 1986; Christiansen and Reinert 1990). Adult males are easy to identify because of their light-gray plumage, but adult females and juveniles may often be lumped together as "brown birds" if they are observed only from a great distance or under poor lighting conditions. For nesting surveys, the practical approach is to drive all available roads through open habitat areas watching for adult birds (Call 1978). Adults will return to the nest quite often with food and may reveal the general location of the nest. Systematic searches through the suspected area may reveal the nest or flush the adults from the site. Harrier

Adult male Northern Harrier.

nests are very susceptible to ground predators, so nest searches should be conducted only for professional research activities.

Conservation and Management. Nests are easily destroyed on farmland as a result of livestock (trampling), haying, early mowing, burning, plowing, and other agricultural practices. Destruction of freshwater and estuarine wetlands has also impacted breeding and wintering harrier populations. No specific conservation measures have been taken, but harriers certainly benefit from waterfowl and upland gamebird management, with programs like the National Wildlife Refuge system (MacWhirter and Bildstein 1996). In open areas prone to rapid reforestation, prescibed burning and grazing have been suggested to prevent forest succession (Serrentino 1987).

A juvenile Northern Harrier hunts on the wing.

A juvenile Northern Harrier banking on one of its low quartering flights.

SHARP-SHINNED HAWK (*Accipiter striatus*)
Length 10.5"; Wingspan 21"

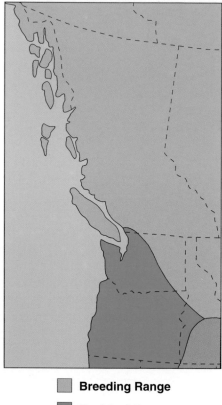

Breeding Range

Resident Range

Adult Sharp-shinned Hawk hidden in a thicket watching a bird feeder.

Range. The Sharp-shinned Hawk breeds from sea level to nearly 11,000 feet (3,350 m) in coastal and interior forests of the Pacific Northwest. This forest hawk breeds throughout British Columbia (Godfrey 1986) where nesting occurs from sea level up to 8,500 feet (2,600 m) in elevation, but generally at higher elevations above 3,400 feet (900 m) (Campbell et al. 1990). Washington GAP Analysis records show most breeding in the Cascades, northeastern forests, and Blue Mountains (Smith et al. 1997). In Oregon, they breed throughout all forested regions including the Coast range, Cascades, Klamath Mountains, and Blue Mountains (Csuti et al. 1997). The species

overwinters throughout the region, but many individuals are also migratory. This is the most migratory species of the three Accipiters (Reynolds 1989).

Status. The status of this small forest hawk has been of some concern, but so far, there are no significant data to prove that it is in decline. All western states (9) described them as a common to fairly common resident, but little data was available to assess population trends of this secretive forest raptor (Reynolds 1989). Population declines were not observed for BBS Routes in Oregon and Washington National Forests during the period encompassing 1968 to 1989 (Sharp 1992). The Sharp-shin appeared on the Blue List from 1972 to 1986, remaining "very rare as a breeder" according to Tate (1986), but it has no special state, federal, or provincial status in the Pacific Northwest.

Habitat Requirements. Sharp-shinned Hawks usually nest in young (25-50 years old), dense stands of even-aged conifers that have high canopy closure, many lower dead limbs (self-pruning), sparse ground cover, and shady, cool conditions (Moore and Henny 1983; Reynolds 1983). These young conifer stands are in the stem exclusion stage which results in a dense single-storied stand (averaging 478 trees per acre or 193 trees per ha), with a shallow crown (Reynolds 1983). Evidence indicates that this hawk might be a forest interior species. Rosenberg and Raphael (1986) found that the species was positively correlated with stand area and area of adjacent hardwoods, but negatively correlated with the percentage of clearcuts.

Nesting. Nesting occurs most frequently in submature conifers, but deciduous trees are sometimes used. Dense conifers provide concealment of the nest against aerial predators (Reynolds 1989) such as Great Horned Owls, Northern Goshawks, and Red-tailed Hawks and scavengers (egg predators) such as crows and ravens. Nest trees averaged 16.2 inches (41.1 cm) in diameter and 89 feet (27.1 m) in height in the Oregon Coast Range (Reynolds et al. 1982). In eastern Oregon, nest trees were smaller, averaging 9.1 inches (23.1 cm) in diameter and 36 feet (11.0 m) in height (Reynolds et al. 1982). Nest trees averaged 11.3 inches (28.7 cm) in diameter in the Wallowa-Whitman National Forest of

Adult Sharp-shinned Hawk in flight.

Oregon and 20% of nests were built on mistletoe (Moore and Henny 1983). Nests are usually situated on north-facing slopes and are often associated with a watercourse (Reynolds et al. 1982). Sharp-shinned Hawks avoided southern and southeastern slopes for nesting in the Wallowa-Whitman National Forest (Moore and Henny 1983).

Eggs and Young. The eggs are usually white to bluish-white and irregularly blotched with browns (Godfrey 1986) and average 1.5 x 1.2 inches (38.1 x 30.5 mm) in size (Herron et al. 1985). In Oregon, clutch size averaged 4.6 and productivity averaged 2.7 young per nesting attempt (Reynolds and Wight 1978). In British Columbia, dates for 12 broods ranged from 3 July to 12 August (Campbell et al. 1990).

Hunting Behavior and Diet. Sharp-shinned Hawks feed primarily on small birds, but will occasionally take small mammals (<5%) as prey (Reynolds 1989). Platt (1973) defined three types of foraging strategies used by these hawks. With "prospect flight", the hawk would leave a perch, make a few gliding circles 3 to 20 feet (1 to 7 m) above ground to inspect the area for small birds, and then land on a

Adult Sharp-shinned Hawk.

different perch. With "still hunting" a hawk perched patiently on a single perch waiting for prey to show up. With "speculative hunting", the hawk would fly just above ground at a fast rate of speed, presumably to startle, flush, or ambush prey that are spotted while flying.

Territory and Density. Sharp-shinned Hawks maintain fairly large home ranges for their comparatively small size. Home ranges of breeding individuals have been estimated to range from 160-1,000 acres (65 to 405 ha) (Johnsgard 1990). In Wyoming, two pairs were estimated to range between 166-326 acres (67.2 and 131.9 ha) during the nesting season based on visual sightings (Craighead and Craighead 1956). In Oregon, Reynolds and Wight (1978) located 4 nests on a 11,741 ha study area for a density of 1 nest per 6,793 acres (2,750 ha) and the mean distance between nests was 2.6 miles (4.3 km) (Reynolds and Wight 1978). Wintering birds in an urban area of southwestern Idaho showed some fidelity by returning after two years and sometimes three years in a row (Powers 1996).

Juvenile Sharp-shinned Hawk in flight.

Survey Methods. Nests can be found by systematically searching entire pre-designated study areas on foot (Reynolds et al. 1982) and by looking for sign such as plucking posts (with prey remains), eggshells, molted feathers, whitewash, protesting adults, or begging juveniles. Broadcasts of taped calls have been used to facilitate searches for active Sharp-shin nests in potential nesting stands (Wiggers and Kritz 1994).

Conservation and Management. Call (1978) thought that stand size had to be a minimum of at least 4 hectares (10 acres) for successful nesting. For conservation of breeding habitat for all *Accipiters*, Jones (1979) recommended that riparian zones up to 1,312 feet (400 m) on either side of the stream should be left undisturbed and nest sites should be protected by not allowing disturbances within 1,312 to 1,640 feet (400 to 500 m). Reynolds (1983) recommended uncut areas around nest sites of at least 10 acres (4 ha) for Sharp-shinned Hawks with a density of at least 20 sites per township (36 square miles or 93.2 square km).

Juvenile Sharp-shinned Hawk.

COOPER'S HAWK (*Accipiter cooperii*)
Length 15.5"; Wingspan 28"

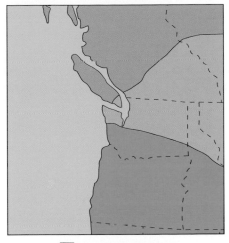

Adult Cooper's Hawk in flight.

■ **Breeding Range**

■ **Resident Range**

Range. In Oregon, the Cooper's Hawk breeds throughout all forested regions including the Coast range, Cascades, Klamath Mountains, and Blue Mountains (Csuti et al. 1997). In Washington, it breeds throughout forested regions of the state, but is noticeably rare along the coastal forests (Smith et al. 1997). The Cooper's Hawk breeds at lower and middle elevations and is absent from high elevations due to a lack of hardwood trees (Smith et al. 1997). In British Columbia, Cooper's Hawks breed in the southern one-third of the Province and southern half of Vancouver Island (Godfrey 1986). Nesting occurs from sea level up to 3,700 feet (1,130 m) in elevation in British Columbia (Campbell et al. 1990).

Adult Cooper's Hawk portrait.

Throughout this range, Cooper's Hawks may overwinter, but may also be migratory.

Status. The Cooper's Hawk may have suffered some slight declines in recent times, but evidence is far from conclusive. While recent population declines were significant at Oregon and Washington National Forests, significant decreases were not evident when data was analyzed individually on a statewide basis (Sharp 1992). Suspected population declines have been primarily attributed to the loss of lowland riparian forests. Pesticide contamination may have contributed to declines, especially on the wintering grounds in Mexico. Shooting is no longer considered a significant threat in the United States or Canada, but is still a common event in Mexico (Rosenfield and Bielefeldt 1993). In the Pacific Northwest, the Cooper's Hawk has no special state, federal, or provincial status.

Habitat Requirements. The Cooper's Hawk most often nests in young to mid-successional stage even-aged conifer forest (30-70 years old), deciduous riparian forest (red alder, aspen, birch, cottonwood), or mixed conifer-hardwood stands, usually near streams or other open water (Reynolds 1983; Smith et al. 1997; Campbell et al. 1990). These forests range from extensive wilderness to smaller forest fragments, woodlots, deciduous riparian groves, small conifer plantations, and suburban habitats (Reynolds 1983; Rosenfield and Bielefeldt 1993). This woodland hawk may occur deep within contiguous forest, but it is not generally considered a true forest interior species. Cooper's Hawks often nest in fragmented forest where forest edge and non-forested habitats are prevalent (Rosenfield and Bielefeldt 1993).

Nesting. The nests are crow-sized, built in the crotch of deciduous trees or at the base of limb axils of conifers usually concealed within the canopy layer (Reynolds et al. 1982). The nest tree is usually a medium-

Juvenile Cooper's Hawk in flight.

sized tree belonging to the submature or mature age class. Nest trees averaged 17.2 inches (43.7 cm) in diameter in the Wallowa-Whitman National Forest of Oregon where most (64.5%) were built on mistletoe platforms (Moore and Henny 1983). Nest trees averaged 13.1 inches (33.3 cm) in diameter and 73 feet (22.2 m) in height in the Oregon Coast Range (Reynolds et al. 1982). In eastern Oregon, nest trees averaged 15.6 inches (39.6 cm) in diameter and 74 feet (22.6 m) in height (Reynolds et al. 1982). Cooper's Hawks avoided southern and southeastern slopes for nesting in the Wallowa-Whitman National (Moore and Henny 1983).

Eggs and Young. The eggs are greenish-white, unmarked or slightly spotted with brown (Godfrey 1986) and approximately 1.9 x 1.5 inches (48.3 x 38.1 mm) in size (Herron et al. 1985). In Oregon, Reynolds and Wight (1978) reported an average clutch size of 3.8 eggs for 13 nests. Egg dates for 38 clutches in British Columbia ranged from 27 April to 24 June and clutch size ranged from 2 to 5 eggs, with 76% having 3 or 4 eggs (Campbell et al. 1990). Brood size (n=37) ranged from 1 to 5 young, with 59% having 3 or 4 young.

Hunting Behavior and Diet. Cooper's Hawks hunt for birds and small mammals in both wooded and open shrubby habitats. In the Bly Mountains of eastern Oregon, they took nearly equal numbers of mammals and birds as prey (60 vs. 53 individuals), but birds were more common than mammals in the diet (202 vs. 73) in the Coast Range near Corvallis (Reynolds and Meslow 1984). Prey is hunted primarily by still-hunting from perches followed by fairly short attack flights, but extended searching flights along woodland edges or through forest may be taken to flush or surprise prey (Johnsgard 1990).

Territory and Density. Cooper's Hawks have fairly large home ranges and breed at relatively low densities for a medium-sized hawk. In Wyoming, one pair was estimated to occupy a home range of at least 506 acres (205 ha) based on visual sightings (Craighead and Craighead 1956). In Oregon, Reynolds and Wight (1978) located 4 nests on a 22,931-acre (9,284-ha) study area for a density of 1 nest per 5,733 acres (2,321 ha) and the mean distance between nests was 2.9 miles (4.7 km).

Survey Methods. Nests can be located by conducting systematic searches on foot of entire pre-designated study areas (Reynolds et al. 1982), and by looking for sign such as plucking posts (with prey remains), eggshells, molted feathers, whitewash, protesting adults, or begging juveniles. Broadcasts of taped calls have been used to facilitate searches of potential nesting stands for active Cooper's Hawk nests (Rosenfield et al. 1985, 1988; Wiggers and Kritz 1994).

Conservation and Management. Cooper's Hawks exhibit the most flexibility in habitat choice of the three North American Accipiters (Reynolds 1983). Stands of closed-canopy trees (30-70 years old) appear to provide optimum breeding habitat. For all *Accipiters*, Jones (1979) recommended that riparian zones up to 1,312 feet (400 m) on either side of the stream should be left undisturbed and nest sites should be protected by not allowing disturbances within 1,312 to 1,640 feet (400 to 500 m). Reynolds (1983) recommended uncut areas around nest sites of at least 15 acres (6 ha) for Cooper's Hawks with a density of at least 5 sites per township (36 square miles or 93.2 square km).

Juvenile Cooper's Hawk portrait.

NORTHERN GOSHAWK (*Accipiter gentilis*)
Length 19"; Wingspan 42"

Adult Northern Goshawk perched in an aspen.

laingi, which inhabits coastal rain forests of Vancouver Island, the Queen Charlotte Islands, and the Coast (Campbell et al. 1990). The goshawk is mostly a permanent resident in British Columbia, but immatures and northern birds may display some migration, and periodically, large numbers may move south (called periodic irruptions) as a result of cyclic fluctuations in prey populations (Campbell et al. 1990).

Resident Range

Wintering Range

Range. In Oregon, the *atricapillus* subspecies breeds throughout the Cascade Range, Blue Mountains, and Klamath Mountains (Reynolds 1989), and only rarely in the Coast Range (DeStefano and McCloskey 1997). In Washington, *A. g. atricapillus* breeds most commonly along the eastern Cascades, but can be found in most mid- to high-elevation forests (Smith et al. 1997). Breeding density appears to increase further inland at higher elevations with very few records from the lowlands on the coast. Goshawks breed throughout forested regions in British Columbia (Godfrey 1986) up to elevations of about 7,500 feet (2,290 m) including the Queen Charlotte race of the goshawk, *A. g.*

Status. In a review of all western states, only California and Nevada suggested that goshawk populations were declining (Reynolds 1989). However, Marshall (1992a) considered the species to be depleted in Oregon, but remaining fairly common in suitable habitat at low densities. Goshawk population declines in California were attributed primarily to the loss and fragmentation of mature and old-growth conifer forests from timber harvesting (Bloom et al. 1986). In Oregon the goshawk was classified as a sensitive species (Marshall 1992a) and it is currently considered a state candidate species in Washington. The *atricapillus* subspecies is currently considered a species of concern by the U.S. Fish and Wildlife Service. In British Columbia, only the *laingi* subspecies is Red-Listed.

Habitat Requirements. Nesting occurs most often in mature and old-growth forest conditions with high canopy closure and usually with a dominance of conifers (Shuster 1980; Hall 1984; Hayward and Escano 1989; Reynolds et al. 1982), although younger forests are sometimes used. On a private industrial forest in the western Washington Cascades, three nests were found in stands ranging from 40 to 54 years old (Bosakowski et al. 1999). Because of their large body size and wing span, goshawks do not usually use younger, dense forests (Fischer 1986) and clearcuts are usually avoided (Iverson et al. 1996). Fleming (1987) noted that 42 percent of nest sites in the Washington Cascades occurred in small sawtimber stands, although trunk or mistletoe deformities were generally needed to support the large, bulky nest which is often too big to be supported by conifers in this size class. In Idaho Douglas-fir forests, goshawks required stands with a minimum average diameter at breast height (DBH) of 10 inches (Lilieholm et al. 1993). Of 31 nest sites examined by Fleming (1987) in western Washington, all were in merchantable timber stands with an average mean stand DBH of 19.1 inches (48.5 cm), minimum mean stand DBH of 9.7 inches (24.6 cm), and average canopy closure of 60 percent. In northern California, Austin (1993) found with telemetry that while 4 of 5 seral stages were used by goshawks, only closed-canopy mature/old-growth forest was used preferentially (more than expected based upon availability). In Oregon, one study found no significant difference in habitat between nests that were found fortuitously and those found during systematic searches (Daw et al. 1998). These results diminish concern that previous research was biased toward finding nests primarily in mature and old-growth forest.

Nesting. The large nest is usually built in a large mature or old-growth tree about halfway to two-thirds the way up, near the bottom of the canopy. The nest is usually placed in either a limb axil, broken leader, or mistletoe platform of a conifer or in a primary or quadruple crotch of a deciduous tree (Bosakowski 1999). With regard to tree species, 30 nests in western Washington were in Douglas-fir and one nest was in a red alder (Fleming 1987). In central British Columbia, nests were more often in conifers with 3 in Douglas-fir, 3 in lodgepole pine, and only 2 in aspens (Bosakowski and Rithaler 1997), albeit conifers were more numerous in the study region. In that area, nest trees averaged 14.0 inches (35.5 cm) in diameter and nest heights averaged 40.3 feet (12.3 meters) above ground. Nest sites are usually situated on north-facing slopes of slight to moderate incline (Reynolds 1983; Hall 1984; Bosakowski ct al. 1999).

Eggs and Young. The eggs are pale bluish-white, unmarked (Godfrey 1986) and approximately 2.3 x 1.8 inches (58.4 x 45.7 mm) in size (Herron et al. 1985). In Oregon, Reynolds and Wight (1978) reported an average clutch size of 3.2 eggs for 48 nests. Egg dates for 5 clutches in British Columbia

Northern Goshawk nest in lodgepole pine near Enterprise, British Columbia.

Juvenile Northern Goshawk.

ranged from 7 April to 15 July, clutch size ranged from 2 to 4 eggs (with 3 clutches having 3 eggs), and brood size for 22 broods ranged from 1 to 4 young, with 11 broods having 2 young (Campbell et al. 1990).

Hunting Behavior and Diet. Goshawks feed on a wide variety of prey species in the Pacific Northwest including: Ruffed Grouse, Blue Grouse, Spruce Grouse, Steller's Jays, Northern Flickers, thrushes, woodpeckers, snowshoe hares, tree squirrels, ground squirrels, chipmunks and various rodents (Reynolds and Meslow 1984; Bull and Hohmann 1994; Watson et al. 1998). On a percent biomass basis, goshawk diets were dominated by grouse (Blue and Ruffed, 43.2%) and showshoe hare (32.6%) in western Washington, and similar results were found for eastern Washington for grouse (39.6%) and hares (40.6%) (Watson et al. 1998). Although by frequency, Douglas squirrels were the most numerous mammal species taken in both eastern and western Washington. Goshawks most often use a short-stay perch hunting technique, flying to new perches every few minutes.

Females will occasionally launch attacks while brooding young on the nest.

Territory and Density. The home range required by a pair of goshawks has been summarized for North America as an area averaging 6,000 acres (2,428 ha), including nest areas of about 30 acres (12 ha), post-fledging family areas averaging about 420 acres (170 ha), and foraging areas of about 5,400 acres (2,185 ha) (Reynolds et al. 1992). Because of these large home ranges, Northern Goshawks typically breed at low

Adult Northern Goshawk portrait.

Juvenile Northern Goshawk in flight.

Conservation and Management.
Management recommendations prepared by
the U.S. Forest Service (Reynolds et al. 1992)
separate the home range into three categories:
a 30-acre nest area (12 ha) consisting of late
seral-stage forest with a dense canopy; a
defended 420-acre post-fledgling-family area
(170 ha) consisting of a variety of forest types
and conditions; and a 5,400-acre foraging
area (2,185 ha) surrounding the core, also
consisting of a variety of forest types and
conditions. U.S. Forest Service management
recommendations include retaining three suitable and three replacement no-harvest 30-
acre nest areas within each goshawk home
range; and suitable canopy cover and forest
structure within the post-fledgling and foraging areas (Reynolds et al. 1992). Even on
intensively harvested timberlands in the
Pacific Northwest, goshawks can nest successfully on managed forests (Bosakowski et
al. 1999), and thus, habitat plans should
always include this species.

densities. For example, mixed-conifer forest
in Oregon supported a maximum density of
0.18 pairs per square mile (0.069
pairs/square km) (DeStefano et al. 1994).

Survey Methods. Goshawks are typically
surveyed during the breeding season when
they are least secretive. Nest searches are
usually conducted with historical visits to
areas of previously known nest sites or
records of sightings. If birds are nesting
they will generally respond vocally and
aggressively to the presence of field workers within 330 feet (100 m) of nests (Speiser
and Bosakowski 1991). If the birds are not
seen, surveyors should search for sign such
as whitewash, prey remains, eggshells, and
greenery on the nest. In other areas where
knowledge of goshawk nesting is absent,
systematic surveys with broadcasted vocalizations are used as an aid in finding new
nests. Use of broadcasted goshawk calls
nearly doubled the response rate of
goshawks in Washington (Watson et al.
1999) with 19 responses without calls and
37 responses with calls. Intensive transects
with broadcasted calls given every 984 feet
(300 m) have been used successfully to
locate nesting goshawks (Kennedy and
Stahlecker 1993; Joy et al. 1995). However,
in steep, mountainous terrain, more practical survey designs have been employed,
including louder broadcasts of goshawk
calls with wider spacing (1,574 feet or 480
m) between call stations (Bosakowski and
Vaughn 1996; Bosakowski 1999).

Goshawk nest in a Douglas-fir stand near
Williams Lake in central British Columbia.

RED-SHOULDERED HAWK *(Buteo lineatus)*
Length 16"; Wingspan 40"

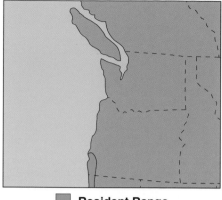

■ **Resident Range**

An adult Red-shouldered Hawk quietly perch hunting from a telephone wire

Range. The western subspecies (*B. l. elegans*) is largely nonmigratory (Bloom 1985) and ranges from central Baja California, through western California, and into southwestern Oregon. A recent range expansion has occurred throughout much of the Oregon Coast Range and Willamette Valley (Henny and Cornely 1985). Elevations below 4,900 feet (1500 m) are preferred in California (Harlow and Bloom 1989).

Status. Populations of this woodland hawk have been stable or increasing in California, and a recent northward range expansion into Oregon suggests that the species may become well-established in the state. Watson et al. (1989) listed no fewer than 7 occurrences in Oregon between 1976 to 1981. Breeding Bird Survey routes suggest that significant population increases have occurred in the *elegans* subspecies, although Crocoll (1994) warns that BBS data are inaccurate for species with large territories. From 1952 to 1967, Christmas Bird Counts showed a stable trend for the California population (Brown 1971). Currently, the species is not listed in California (Bloom et al. 1993) or Oregon, and has no federal status.

Habitat Requirements. This is a woodland raptor that has apparently adapted to urbanization. Local pairs have become quite tame, breeding in residential areas, parks, and cemeteries (Harlow and Bloom 1989). Radiotagged birds in California had home ranges with 39% woodland, 41% coastal sage, and 16% grassland (Bloom et al. 1993). Woodland types used were oak, willow, and sycamore, which were used significantly more than availability. Of 170 nesting territories, 17.6% were considered to be urban (>50%) nesting areas (Bloom and McCrary 1996).

Nesting. The nest is usually built high in a tall mature deciduous tree, but there is little information on nest site selection in

Oregon. Urban Red-shoulders in California nested in western sycamore (52.9%) and coast live oak (10.4%), but also in non-native trees including eucalyptus (32.5%), fan palm (3.9%), and deodara cedar (1.3%) (Bloom and McCrary 1996).

Eggs and Young. The eggs are dull white or faint bluish overlaid with brown and lavender blotches and markings (Crocoll 1994) and average 2.2 x 1.7 inches (54.7 x 43.9 mm) in size (Bent 1937). In California, the average clutch size was 2.7 for a sample of 29 nests and reproductive success was 1.3 fledglings per nest (Wiley 1975).

Hunting Behavior and Diet. Data are scarce for the Northwest, but eastern Red-shoulders eat mostly small mammals, small birds, frogs, snakes, turtles, and occasional insects (Bosakowski and Smith 1992). Hunting is most often done from a low to moderate perch, but soaring and

An adult Red-shouldered Hawk soaring with outstretched wings and tail, note the banded tail and crescent shaped "windows" at the base of the wing tips.

flapping flight sometimes precede an attack on prey.

Territory and Density. Red-shouldered Hawks maintain small breeding territories, but are highly territorial. In California,

A juvenile Red-shouldered Hawk perches atop a telephone pole.

FRANK SCHLEICHER

An adult Red-shouldered Hawk uses a traffic signpost as a hunting perch.

average home range size for radiotagged males was 298 acres (121 ha) and 249 acres (101 ha) for females (Bloom et al. 1993). Although fairly tolerant of most human activities, some adults have been known to aggressively attack humans that stray too close to active nests. In California, no fewer than six adults have been trapped and removed following complaints from people who sustained head injuries from Red-shouldered Hawk attacks (Bloom and McCrary 1996).

Survey Methods. In accordance with their territorial nature, Red-shoulders are highly vocal during the breeding season and will readily protest if people walk near an active nest. Broadcasts of conspecific calls or other raptors (heterospecific calls) can also be used to increase detection rates (Mosher et al. 1990; Bosakowski and Smith 1998). Nests can be located following the procedures of Craighead and Craighead (1956) by driving available roads or walking through woodlots and examining nest structures for signs of activity (greenery, whitewash, feathers, eggshells, prey remains).

Conservation and Management. Loss of riparian and oak woodlands were considered detrimental to Red-shouldered Hawks in California (Harlow and Bloom 1989), thus New Forestry and other conservative logging practices should be beneficial to this hawk. Because of their small territory size and tolerance for human activities, Bloom et al. (1993) recommended well-planned parks, open space, and sanctuaries with at least 300 acres (121 ha) of mosaic habitats (>39% wooded) per pair.

BROAD-WINGED HAWK *(Buteo platypterus)*
Length 13"; Wingspan 33"

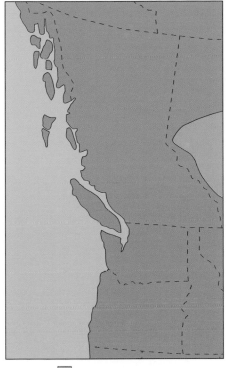

Breeding Range

Adult Broad-winged Hawk perched on telephone wire.

Range. The Broad-winged Hawk breeds just east of British Columbia in Alberta, although since 1965 there have been at least 21 sightings in British Columbia (Campbell et al. 1990) and another recent sighting by one of the authors near Jacobie Lake (Bosakowski and Rithaler 1997). Two records exist for Washington during migratory time periods including an adult sighting during fall in Newport (Larrison 1977) and an immature specimen collected during spring of 1975 in Tacoma (Clark and Anderson 1984). Watson et al. (1989) listed 3 occurrences of the Broad-wing in Oregon including, a subadult photographed in May of 1983 on Malheur NWR in southeastern Oregon (Littlefield 1990), an immature at Malheur in October of 1983, and an immature on the edge of the Coast Range in Washington County in

August of 1983. The Broad-wing is considered a true neotropical migrant, and hence this highly migratory raptor is absent from the Pacific Northwest from late September to late April (Campbell et al. 1990). Migrating birds are extremely gregarious in eastern North America (Goodrich et al. 1996).

Status. This medium-sized *Buteo* is Red-Listed in British Columbia, not because it is declining, but simply because of its rarity in the region. The species was probably never abundant in the Province because it is near the edge of its range in this region, and sightings are considered extralimital (Campbell et al. 1990).

Habitat Requirements. The Broad-winged Hawk is a woodland raptor that generally breeds in contiguous deciduous or mixed woodlands (Goodrich et al. 1996). In Alberta, most Broadwings were sighted in or adjacent to large blocks of forest cover (Rusch and Doerr 1972). Generally, nests are distant from human dwellings, but small canopy openings and wet areas are often used as hunting sites (Goodrich et al. 1996).

Nesting. The nest is typically built in a deciduous or coniferous tree about 20-40

feet (6 to 12 m) above ground (Godfrey 1986). Across North America, average nest tree diameters ranged from 9.8 to 21.3 inches (25 to 54 cm) depending on geographic location (Goodrich et al. 1996) indicating that submature and mature forests are most frequently used for nesting. The stick nest is usually rather small, flimsy, and crudely constructed compared to other hawks its size, although it sometimes refurbishes nests of other raptors and crows. The nest cup is sparsely lined with bark and mosses (Godfrey 1986), and green sprigs may be added to the nest cup and rim – although not incorporated into the nest structure (Goodrich et al. 1996).

Eggs and Young. The eggs are variable in color from ground white, pale creamy, to slightly bluish, blotched or spotted with reddish-brown or purple spots (Godfrey 1986; Goodrich et al. 1996), and approximately 1.9 x 1.5 inches (48.9 x 39.3 mm) in size (Bent 1937). In Alberta, clutch size ranged from 2 to 3 eggs, with 3 clutches having 2 eggs and two having 3 eggs, and productivity was 2.0 young fledged per nest attempt (Rusch and Doerr 1972).

Hunting Behavior and Diet. The Broad-winged Hawk hunts mainly below the canopy from perches where it sits quietly, scanning for prey (Goodrich et al. 1996) and is often quite tame if approached (Bent 1937; TB, DGS). Perch sites are often within 15 feet (5 m) of the ground in a live tree, snag, or telephone wire. However, it occasionally hunts from the wing while soaring or flap-gliding.

A soaring adult Broad-winged Hawk.

In Alberta, mammals represented 62% of the diet, followed by birds (27%), amphibians (9%), and insects (2%) (Rusch and Doerr 1972). Red-backed voles (24%) and meadow voles (19%), and mice (10%) accounted for most of the mammals taken. In addition, the Broadwing is one of the few raptors that consistently preys upon toads which are too noxious for most other birds of prey (Bent 1937; Bosakowski and Smith 1992).

Territory and Density. Broad-wings are territorial and occupy a fairly large home range. They will often defend their territory against the larger Red-tailed Hawk with spectacular aerial battles (TB), but may overlap breeding home ranges of the larger *Buteo* (Goodrich et al. 1996). In Alberta, maximum nesting density for two pairs was 1,373 acres (556 ha) per pair (Rusch and Doerr 1972).

Survey Methods. In Alberta, teams of 2 to 6 field workers systematically traversed wooded areas at intervals of less than 100 feet (30 m) (Rusch and Doerr 1972). Broad-winged Hawks also respond well to high-volume broadcasts of conspecific and heterospecific calls (Bosakowski and Smith 1998) which can help increase detection rates (Mosher et al. 1990).

Conservation and Management. The Broad-wing should be considered in timber management plans (Nelson and Titus 1988), as it seems to prefer large patches of contiguous forest habitat. It has been speculated that short timber rotations (<40 years) may not be adequate to support this species in southeastern forests (Mitchell and Millsap 1990).

Juvenile Broad-winged Hawk perch-hunting from a low wire.

SWAINSON'S HAWK (*Buteo swainsoni*)

Length 18"; Wingspan 49"

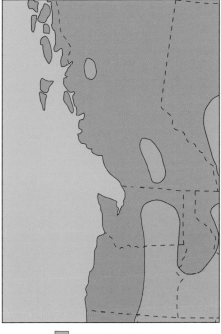

Adult light-morph Swainson's Hawk.

Breeding Range

Range. In British Columbia, this hawk breeds locally in the southern plains of Okanagan Landing and Valley, Dog Creek, Chilcotin River, Telegraph Creek, and Atlin (Godfrey 1986) and Thompson and Nicola River Valleys, and Bulkley Basin from elevations of 1,100-1,500 feet (335 to 457 meters) (Campbell et al. 1990). In Oregon and Washington, it breeds east of the Cascade Mountains in the open, arid shrub-steppe habitat and agricultural lands (Harlow and Bloom 1989). This neotropical migrant arrives in late April and May and departs by late August and early September and was formerly observed migrating in huge flocks (Campbell et al. 1990). At Malheur NWR in southeastern Oregon, average spring arrival is 5 April, with peak migration between 10 and 25 April (Littlefield 1990).

Status. Declines have been reported or suspected in some parts of the Pacific Northwest, including Oregon and British Columbia. Breeding Bird Survey routes on Pacific Northwest National Forests have indicated no significant trends from 1968 to 1989, although it was only detected on seven routes (Sharp 1992). This hawk has declined as a breeding species at Malheur NWR in southeastern Oregon since the 1950s (Littlefield et al. 1984; Littlefield 1990). Several explanations for their decline have been proposed including: pesticide contamination, prey reduction on South American wintering grounds, shooting on the wintering grounds, and habitat loss on nesting and wintering grounds (Harlow and Bloom 1989). An increase in perching habitat (spreading junipers, homesteads, and utility poles) may favor the Red-tailed Hawk at the expense of Swainson's Hawks (Janes 1985, 1987). This species was considered a species of special concern in

Adult light-morph Swainson's Hawk soaring near Richland in eastern Washington.

Oregon and Washington, and declining in Oregon, but stable in Washington (Harlow and Bloom 1989). In British Columbia, the species is currently Red-Listed.

Habitat Requirements. The Swainson's Hawk is a large, soaring *Buteo* hawk which breeds in wide-open country and avoids forested terrain. In north-central Oregon (Morrow County), these hawks nested in juniper-grassland habitat (Green and Morrison 1983). In southeastern Washington, 67 nesting territories were surrounded by wheatland (50.4%), native grassland (25.2%), and shrub vegetation (17.2%) within a 1.9 mile (3 km) radius around nest sites (Bechard et al. 1990).

Nesting. The Swainson's Hawk nests in a variety of small to large trees, usually avoiding dead trees (snags) or live trees with dead tops. In a southeastern Washington study area, all 67 nests were located in trees (black locust, box elder, willow, ponderosa pine, and juniper) and average nest height above ground was 38 feet (11.6 m) (Bechard et al. 1990). In north-central Oregon, 14 nests were in junipers (avg. 20.3 feet or 6.2 m) and nest height averaged only 15.4 feet (4.7 m) above ground (Green and Morrison 1983). At Malheur NWR in southeastern Oregon, 18 nests were all in western junipers with an average nest tree height of 18 feet (5.5 m) and average nest height of 16.4 feet (5.0 m) (Johnstone in Littlefield et al. 1984). In

British Columbia, 9 of 14 nests were in conifers including ponderosa pine (7), Douglas-fir (1) and spruce (1) and nest heights ranged from 15 to 75 feet (4.6 to 23 m) above ground (Campbell et al. 1990). The nest is often small and flimsy compared to Red-tailed Hawk nests, composed of weed stems and small branches, and often blows-out during wind storms (Call 1978). These hawks are quite trusting and often nest close to houses and buildings (Call 1978). In one study area in northern Utah, the average distance of nests to buildings was only 820 feet (250 m) (Bosakowski et al. 1996).

Eggs and Young. The eggs are pale bluish to dull white, usually marked sparingly and irregularly with brown (Godfrey 1986) and approximately 2.2 x 1.7 inches (56.5 x 44 mm) in size (Bent 1937). In British Columbia, egg dates for 7 clutches ranged from 10 May to 1 July and clutch size ranged from 1 to 4 eggs (Campbell et al. 1990). In Washington, Fitzner (1978) reported an average clutch size of 2.18 eggs. Brood size (n=10) ranged from 1 to 4 young, with 8 having 2 young in British Columbia (Campbell et al. 1990).

Hunting Behavior and Diet. In northern Utah, the diet was comprised of mammals (52%), insects (31%), and birds (17%) (Smith and Murphy 1973). In Washington, insects were an insignificant part of the diet, which included a substantial amount of

Adult dark-morph Swainson's Hawk soaring.

A light-morph Swainson's Hawk hunting from a fence post.

jackrabbits and cottontails, and a variety of rodents, birds, reptiles, and toads (Fitzner 1978). Although the Swainson's Hawk frequently forages from perches, it uses aerial foraging (soaring) to a greater extent than Red-tailed Hawks (Janes 1985). Low perches less than 7 feet (2 m) are used more often (59.7%) than higher perches for hunting (Janes 1985).

Territory and Density. These hawks are very territorial and nests are often regularly spaced on the landscape as a result. In southeastern Washington, mean nearest-neighbor distance was 1.46 miles (2.36 km) (Bechard et al. 1990). In northern Utah, mean nearest-neighbor distance was 1.08 mile (1.74 km) and nesting density was 0.26 nests per square mile or 0.10 nests per square km (Bosakowski et al. 1996). Most pairs are non-aggressive, but several times adults have swooped at the authors while walking below active nests. Generally, the adults wait until your back is turned and then they silently swoop down, and at the last second, they bank steeply upwards while "ruffling" their wings. This ruffling is quite loud and startling, but the birds did not attempt to strike us. However, we have heard of a nest in Logan, Utah where the adults regularly struck bicyclists who rode past a roadside nest.

Survey Methods. Nests are easily detected by driving available roads in desert and agricultural valleys and searching tree tops with binoculars (Call 1978). The presence of adult birds is a helpful hint to intensify nest searching (Bosakowski et al. 1996). When adults are found, they can be carefully watched from a distance and will sometimes reveal the nest location when returning with nesting material or food. Approaching adults on foot can also sometimes reveal a nest because the adults will utter protesting screams, circle the nest site, and sometimes stoop at intruders if they are within 100 yards (100 m) of a nest (Call 1978; TB, DGS).

Conservation and Management. Erection of artificial nest platforms has been shown to significantly increase nesting density in an area (Schmutz et al. 1984). However, these open-topped sites are more often used by Red-tailed and Ferruginous Hawks (England et al. 1997), and thus, tree plantings may be a better long-range management alternative (Fitzner 1980). Attempts to make powerlines "user-friendly" have been carried-out to reduce the risk of electrocution to open country raptors that use these structures for perches (Olendorff et al. 1981). Habitat loss is occurring through economic conversion of agricultural areas to commercial and residential real estate (Bosakowski et al. 1996; England et al. 1997) and possibly overgrazing.

RED-TAILED HAWK *(Buteo jamaicensis)*
Length 18"; Wingspan 48"

Advanced fledgling Red-tailed Hawk
(flightless) near Yakima Canyon,
Eastern Washington.

TOM BOSAKOWSKI

■ Breeding Range

■ Resident Range

Range. In British Columbia, Godfrey
(1986) shows the entire province as breeding range, where it breeds up to 7,300 feet
(2,230 m) in elevation (Campbell et al.
1990). The Washington GAP Analysis
shows that the breeding range occurs
throughout the state, but generally absent
from dense coastal rain forests on the
westside of the Olympic Peninsula (Smith
et al. 1997). In Oregon, the Red-tailed
Hawk breeds throughout the state (Csuti et
al. 1997). Within the Northwest Region,
the Red-tail is a partial short-distance
migrant. Migration may occur in some
individuals, but is not known how many
residents leave their territories and how

many birds from the north may migrate
into the region. The major wintering area
in British Columbia is the Fraser
Lowlands (Campbell et al. 1990).

Status. Red-tail populations have been considered stable in Washington and Oregon
(Harlow and Bloom 1989), and are probably increasing in suburban environments of
British Columbia (Runyan 1987). Recent
population levels from 1986 to 1989 have
been stable on National Forests in Oregon
and Washington (Sharp 1992). Christmas
Bird Count data from British Columbia
indicate a steady increase in numbers
(Campbell et al. 1990).

Habitat Requirements. This large, hardy
raptor is an extreme habitat generalist,

occurring in every habitat, except possibly for dense coastal rain forest. In a rural western Washington county (Snohomish), 27 breeding territories were studied in an area of pastures and cropland (18%), old or fallow fields (59%), and second and third-growth woodlots (23%) (Speiser 1990). On a private industrial forest in the western Washington Cascades (near Morton), Red-tailed Hawk sightings from breeding bird routes were positively correlated with mature conifer stands (>45 years old), but not with other younger habitats that were also abundant (Bosakowski 1997). This suggested that the mature stands were a limiting or critical factor for nest sites, but other habitat types were not limiting to this wide-ranging habitat generalist.

Nesting. The large nest is most often placed high in a tall dominant tree (usually deciduous) in forested areas or on a cliff or transmission tower in open treeless country. In suburbia, nesting often occurs along highways and close to houses. In

Adult Red-tailed Hawk soaring.

developed areas around Seattle, they commonly nest along the I-5 corridor, despite traffic noise and human disturbance (Smith et al. 1997). In one study, 6 of 35 nests were reported near highways less than 330 feet (100 m) (Speiser 1990). On the edge of urban and rural Vancouver, British Columbia, 4 of 22 active nest were within 330 (100 m) of highways, but 5 other nests were located on river islands (Runyan 1987). In Vancouver, all nests were found in deciduous trees including: 11 nests in black cottonwood, five in

Juvenile Red-tailed Hawk perched on power pole.

paper birch, and one each in willow, elm, and black locust (Runyan 1987). Northeast of Seattle, all nests were also built in deciduous trees including, 68% in black cottonwood and the remaining 32% in red alder (Speiser 1990). Since then, at least two nests have been found in conifers (Douglas-firs) in nearby Redmond, Washington (TB). Most woodlots containing nests were larger than 1 hectare (2.5 acres), and only rarely were they in isolated trees and shelterbelts (Speiser 1990). In the open country of southeastern Washington, Red-tailed Hawks nested on cliffs (19), transmission towers (11), and trees (27) (Bechard et al. 1990). Similar results were found in the Esquatzel Coulee area of southeastern Washington, where 9 nests were built on cliffs, one was in a tree, and another was on a transmission tower (Knight and Smith 1982). Outside dimensions of nests in British Columbia ranged from 14.1 to 42.1 inches (36 to 107 cm) in diameter and 9 to 48 inches (23 to 122 cm) in depth (Campbell et al. 1990). The majority of these nests were lined with fresh and old conifer sprigs as well as bark strips, rootlets, mosses, cones, grasses and feathers.

Eggs and Young. The eggs are white, and usually spotted with browns (Godfrey 1986) and approximately 2.3 x 1.8 inches (58.4 x 45.7 mm) in size (Herron et al. 1985). Egg dates for 83 clutches ranged from 28 February to 20 June and clutch size for 81 clutches ranged from 1 to 4 eggs, with 81% having 2 or 3 eggs (Campbell et al. 1990). Brood size (n=237) ranged from 1 to 4 young, with 56% having 2 young (Campbell et al. 1990).

Hunting Behavior and Diet. Red-tailed Hawks are opportunistic, generalist predators with a diverse diet. From a sample of 90 prey items and captures in north-central Oregon, at least 16 species of vertebrates were taken as prey including 66 mammals, 12 snakes, 10 birds, and two beetles (Janes 1984). Hunting occurs most commonly by soaring and subsequent stooping when prey are detected, but still-hunting from an

Adult Red-tailed Hawk.

elevated perch is also used regularly (Johnsgard 1990). In open fields and marshes without suitable perches, Red-tails will use hover hunting to remain stationary in the air as they scan the ground. During strong steady breezes, Red-tails will also use kiting to remain motionless as they hang on strong updrafts without flapping.

Territory and Density. These large hawks are highly territorial and have fairly large home ranges. Surprisingly, one of the highest nesting densities (one nest per 1.39 square miles or 3.6 square km) has been estimated in a suburban-urban area around Vancouver, B.C. (Runyan 1987). In north-central Oregon, Wasco County, 9-10 of 33 pairs lost portions of their territories to later-arriving Swainson's Hawks (Janes 1994). Red-tails can be very active in their defense of young, making numerous "stoops" at any intruders that may approach the nest site (Call 1978). Red-tails from Washington were more likely to respond aggressively (calling and diving) than Red-tails from areas that have been settled longer by humans such as West Virginia, Wisconsin, or California (Knight et al. 1989).

Survey Methods. Surveys are generally conducted by driving available roads and examining nest-like structures in trees or by examining cliff lines with binoculars for the presence of stick nests (Call 1978). In large stands or heavily-forested areas, high-volume broadcasts of conspecific calls can increase detection efforts (Balding and Dibble 1984; Mosher et al. 1990) and may be helpful in pinpointing the location of the nest. Other survey methods discussed for the *Accipiter* hawks would also be applicable for Red-tails occurring in forest situations.

Conservation and Management. Where potential nest sites are scarce, man-made structures such as wooden power poles and steel power towers can provide suitable nest

Red-tailed Hawk nest on Bull Mountain, British Columbia.

sites for Red-tails (Call 1979). Attempts to make these powerlines "user-friendly" have been carried-out to reduce the risk of electrocution by perching raptors in open treeless country (Olendorff et al. 1981). Since the Red-tail is a habitat generalist, there have been few attempts to specifically manage land for their benefit. However, we know of one case where the township of Redmond, Washington, established a 1 hectare (2.5 acres) no-cut zone around a nest in a new townhouse development, but the nest has not been used, at least during the following two years (TB). Most habitat disturbances have resulted in expansion of this habitat generalist (Harlow and Bloom 1989). On private industrial forest land in Morton, Washington, Red-tailed Hawks were common breeding season residents (Bosakowski 1997) since clearcutting has probably allowed them to expand into areas which were densely forested and formerly dominated by Accipiters.

FERRUGINOUS HAWK *(Buteo regalis)*
Length 20"; Wingspan 54"

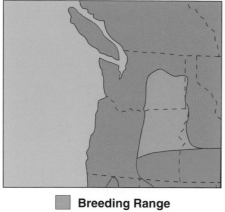

■ **Breeding Range**

■ **Resident Range**

Portrait of an adult Ferruginous Hawk
(light morph).

Range. In the Pacific Northwest, the
Ferruginous Hawk occurs in the Palouse
Prairie regions of southeastern Oregon and
Washington. Today this hawk is mostly
restricted to steppe vegetation of south-central Washington (Kittitas, Yakima, Douglas,
Franklin, Walla Walla, Whitman, and
Columbian counties) along the Snake River,
while in Oregon they are found in similar
habitat east of the Cascades. In British
Columbia it is considered a very rare summer visitor to the southern central interior
and possibly a very local nesting species
(Campbell et al. 1990). Only 13 sightings
(including two nesting records) of this hawk
have been recorded in British Columbia
prior to 1990, all from the south-central part
of the province. This large hawk is a short-
distance migrant, retreating to southern
Oregon and further south for the winter.

Status. The status of the Ferruginous Hawk
in the Pacific Northwest is considered stable
or slowly declining. This hawk has declined
as a breeding species since the 1940s at
Malheur NWR in southern Oregon
(Littlefield 1990). Nevertheless, analysis of
Christmas Bird Count data suggests that the

overall population is not declining, but
rather increasing (Warkentin and James
1988). Furthermore, Breeding Bird Survey
data from 1966 to 1991 showed stability in
continental numbers as well as significantly
more routes reporting increases than
declines (Knopf 1994). In terms of occupied
nests, at least 60 nests in Washington were
known in 1994 and 64 were known in 1987
(Richardson 1996). The species was included on the Blue List from 1972-81 and later
listed as a Species of Special Concern from
1982-86 (Ehrlich et al. 1988). In
Washington, it is listed as a state-threatened
species, and federally, it is considered a
species of concern. In British Columbia, it
is currently Red-Listed.

Habitat Requirements. The Ferruginous
Hawk is an open country bird and is an
obligate grassland or desert-shrub nester.
They occur most commonly in landscapes
dominated by native prairies, steppe grasslands, plains, semiarid deserts, badlands,
haylands, and pasture, but cropland is generally avoided (Richardson 1996). Preferred
vegetation cover in southeastern
Washington includes big sage/fescue,
wheatgrass/fescue, and three tip sage

habitats, all in the southern and central Columbian Basin (Bechard et al. 1990; Smith et al. 1997). Most habitat in Washington is found on private land (79%), with 18% on federal land, and 3% on state land (Richardson 1996).

Nesting. Nests are constructed in low trees, cliffs, rocky outcrops, buttes, and other platforms that provide both unobstructed views of their territory and also provide favorable updrafts or local updrafts that enhance quick takeoffs. If low cliffs or rock outcrops are unavailable a pair may simply construct a nest directly on the ground of a low hill or grassy knoll. Pairs may sometimes resort to nesting on towers and other structures such as haystacks, windmills, chimneys, and artificial nest platforms (Richardson 1996). A small Hanford (Washington) population of 7 to 10 pairs nested on utility towers (8) and trees (2), and foraged in the nearby steppe and irrigated croplands (Fitzner et al. 1992). In southeastern Washington, 72.8% of nests were greater than 1.25 miles (2.0 km) from roads or areas with people (Bechard et al. 1990), displaying their general low tolerance

Ferruginous Hawk nestlings near Yakima Canyon, Washington.

for human disturbance. Nests are constructed of larger branches and shaggy bark of nearby forbs, shrubs and trees and lined with stalks and shreds of dried grasses, roots, cow dung, scraps of paper, miscellaneous trash, and strips of inner bark. Nests may be lined with greenery such as new green leaves or the green twigs of cedars or other conifers, especially later in the courtship and nest building cycle.

Eggs and Young. The eggs are white or pale bluish with brown blotches and spots

Adult Ferruginous Hawk (light morph).

and approximately 2.4 x 1.9 inches (60.9 x 48.3 mm) in size (Herron et al. 1985). Mean clutch size ranged from 1.5 to 4.4 eggs, with most nests having 2 to 4 eggs (Olendorff 1993). In Washington, productivity varied from 1.6 to 2.6 young per active nest (Richardson 1996). Juvenile dispersal occurs an average of 27 days after fledging (Olendorff 1993). Nesting dates for Ferruginous Hawks in eastern Washington range from late March to mid July (Jewett et al. 1953) whereas Bent (1937) records egg dates for this state from 24 March to 10 May.

Adult Ferruginous Hawk (light morph) in flight from Richland, eastern Washington.

Hunting Behavior and Diet. Ferruginous Hawks prey mostly on medium-sized mammals such as cottontails and jackrabbits, ground squirrels, pocket gophers, and mice (Smith and Murphy 1978; Smith et al. 1981; Bechard and Schmutz 1995). An occasional bird is also taken, especially quail, pheasants, and other ground dwelling species although this big hawk will take sparrows and songbirds during migration or while on nests. If mammals are not available or their abundance decreases, Ferruginous Hawks will take a variety of lizards and snakes (Smith and Murphy 1973). Campbell et al. (1990) suggested that pairs nesting in the open country around Okanagan Valley may be feeding on populations of medium-sized mammals such as Columbian ground squirrels, northern pocket gophers, and yellow-bellied

marmots. Ferruginous Hawks typically are crepuscular hunters, working the twilight hours of dawn and dusk in search of a wide variety of vertebrate, and less commonly, invertebrate prey. If food is scarce or hunting conditions are poor, however, they will extend their hunting activities through the late morning and into the mid-afternoon and early evening hours as well. Prey is generally taken via a steep dive, but sometimes these hawks will quarter back and forth in search of prey, or hunt from a low perch. Occasionally, they will alight and run along the ground, or leap after prey on the ground (Smith and Murphy 1973).

Territory and Density. Ferruginous Hawks aggressively defend their territory through aerial displays, postures, and aggressive pursuits of intruders (Smith and Murphy 1973). Home range size in southcentral Washington averaged 19,513 acres (7,900 ha) based on the 95% minimum convex polygon method and 7,657 acres (3,100 ha) using an 85% adaptive kernel estimation (Leary 1996). The actual size of defended home range (territory) is unknown, but there is evident regular spacing of nests across open habitat (Bechard and Schumtz 1995). Evidence of territoriality is further provided by nearest neighbor distances, which averaged 8.3 miles (13.4 km) with a range of 0.5 to 4.5 miles (0.8-7.2 km) between active nests (Olendorff 1993).

Adult dark-morph Ferruginous Hawk in flight.

Ferruginous Hawk nest on a small rocky outcrop near Yakima Canyon, Washington.

Survey Methods. Nests are rather conspicuous while driving available roads in the open country habitats favored by this hawk (Call 1978). Besides looking for nests in trees, powerlines, and other elevated structures, the surveyor should scan rocky outcrops and cliffs with binoculars and spotting scopes (TB, DGS). However, nest sites on the ground should not be overlooked and may require careful systematic coverage of the study area. If adults are observed circling in the sky, a nest is often within a half mile (800 m) (Call 1978). The adults are moderately to highly defensive of their young, and will dive and scream at intruders, although seldom actually striking field workers. During the last two weeks before fledging, nestlings will often stand conspicuously on the edge of the nest to permit better cooling by desert breezes.

Conservation and Management. In terms of habitat protection, residential and agricultural development need to be prevented or mitigated against if occurring within home ranges (Richardson 1996).

Availability of nest sites is often low and can affect the suitability of habitats for nesting. In southcentral Wyoming, 71 artificial nest platforms were erected and between 11 and 41 platforms were used each year with higher nest success and fledging rates than natural nest sites (Tigner et al. 1996). Tree planting may also be an important strategy since Ferruginous Hawks often take advantage of abandoned homesteads by using black locust and other trees originally planted for shade (Richardson 1996). By 1993, no quantitative applied studies had shown detrimental effects of overgrazing on Ferruginous Hawks (Olendorff 1993), but this certainly does not rule-out the possibility on other unstudied lands. Ferruginous Hawks are sensitive to human disturbance factors, often resulting in nest desertion and decreased productivity (Smith and Murphy 1973; White and Thurow 1985). Nest buffers from 820 to 3,600 feet (250 to 1,100 m) have been recommended between 1 March and 15 August (Richardson 1966).

ROUGH-LEGGED HAWK *(Buteo lagopus)*
Length 19"; Wingspan 52"

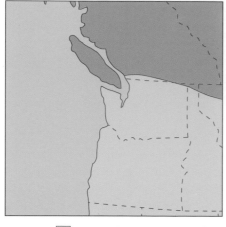

Wintering Range

Close-up of adult light-morph Rough-legged Hawk captured for banding near Ocean Shores, Washington.

Range. The Rough-legged Hawk does not breed anywhere in Oregon, Washington, or British Columbia, but winters throughout the region (Harlow and Bloom 1989). In British Columbia, it is a regular migrant and winter visitant throughout most of the province east of the Coast Ranges, except for the south coast where most (83%) records have been established (Campbell et al. 1990). It has been recorded from sea level to at least 7,000 feet (2,130 m) in elevation (in migration) and the major wintering area is in the Fraser Lowlands (Campbell et al. 1990). Rough-legs usually arrive at Malheur NWR in southeastern Oregon in mid-October with the earliest date of 25 September (Littlefield 1990). Departure in spring is more variable with peak numbers between 1-20 April, and a maximum date of 11 May. Rough-legs usually migrate singly or in small groups, but Hardy (1957) reported two different large groups of 10 and 22 birds.

Status. Wintering populations of this species were considered stable in Oregon and unknown in Washington (Harlow and Bloom 1989). In British Columbia, it is Yellow-Listed indicating a stable population.

Habitat Requirements. In winter and in migration, this hawk prefers open tree-less habitats such as fields, desert, cropland, and marshes (Godfrey 1986). At Malheur NWR, Rough-legs used idle land more than expected at 53%, but used hayed land similar to expected at 25%, and grazed land was used less than expected at 22% (Littlefield et al. 1992). The use of clearcuts for foraging is probable, but not well documented.

Hunting Behavior and Diet. The principal winter diet includes voles and mice, but birds, rabbits, and hares are also taken (Johnsgard 1990). In addition, carrion is often consumed in winter. In Idaho, an increased use of road-killed rabbits occurred during periods of snow cover (Watson 1986). This hawk usually hunts from perches (trees, snags, fence posts, power poles) by the "sit and wait" technique or by soaring and hovering over open ground without available perches. Occasionally, it will also hunt while perched on the ground.

Adult light-morph Rough-legged Hawk soaring.

Adult dark-morph Rough-legged Hawk.

Survey Methods. Winter-time surveys such as the Christmas Bird Count account for most of the data on this wintering hawk (Smith and Knight 1981). At Malheur NWR, a 42-mile (67-km) road transect was driven at about 9 mph (14 kmph) and hawks within 0.75 miles (1.2 km) were counted (Littlefield et al. 1992). Surveys were repeated at approximately two-week intervals.

Conservation and Management. Prevention of overgrazing may have benefits for maintaining adequate small mammal prey populations. At Malheur NWR, studies have suggested that wintering habitat can be protected by reducing or eliminating livestock grazing in meadows and marshes (Littlefield et al. 1992). Management of power line and power pole design to prevent electrocution is also a valuable conservation measure (Olendorff et al. 1981) for this open country raptor.

Light-morph Rough-legged Hawk on nesting grounds at north slope of the Brooks range.

GOLDEN EAGLE (*Aquila chrysaetos*)
Length 32"; Wingspan 78"

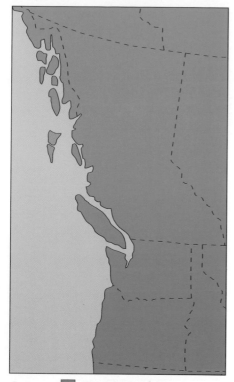

Resident Range

Golden Eagle close-up.

Range. The Golden Eagle is a widely distributed resident throughout western North America, except for the recent extirpation in the Central Valley of California (Harlow and Bloom 1989). In Washington, this species more commonly breeds in the southeastern lowlands and deserts, but nesting has been occurring more frequently in western Washington due to clearcutting forestry practices (Bruce et al. 1982). In British Columbia, Godfrey (1986) shows the entire province as breeding range, except for the Queen Charlotte Islands. Most breeding occurs in mountainous areas, deep river canyons, and large coastal islands from sea level up to 7,800 feet (2,380 m), although most nests have been found between 980 to 4,000 feet (300 to

1,220 m) (Campbell et al. 1990). In Oregon, it also breeds predominantly east of the Cascade Range in open, arid country (Csuti et al. 1997). Northern populations are migratory, and fall movements occur in September and October.

Status. Although numerous cases of mortality are linked to man each year, evidence of a declining population has not been clearly documented in the Pacific Northwest. Environmental problems associated with Golden Eagle populations have been attributed primarily to toxicologic responses to man-made pollutants. Lead toxicosis has recently been identified as potential threat to Golden Eagle populations (Harlow and Bloom 1989). Collisions and electrocutions with powerlines have been another environmental problem affecting Golden Eagle survival in the western United States (Olendorff et al. 1981). Still others are killed illegally each year by irate ranchers and sheep herders or killed incidently by traps and poison set out for other pest species such as coyotes and rodents (Bent 1937; Newton 1979). Approximately 500 breeding pairs were estimated to nest in California (California Department of Fish and Game 1987), but only 80 pairs were estimated for Washington State in 1990 (Rodrick and Milner 1991). The Golden Eagle is not listed as threatened or endangered, but is federally-protected under the "Bald and Golden Recovery Eagle Act." The Golden Eagle is currently considered a candidate species in Washington, but is reported as common by all other western states (Harlow and Bloom 1989).

Habitat Requirements. In the Pacific Northwest, Golden Eagles occupy primarily mountain, desert, and canyon habitats, usually avoiding dense forested areas where hunting is difficult because of their large wingspans (Johnsgard 1990). East of the Cascade Range, they are commonly associated with open, arid sagebrush, ponderosa pine, and grassland habitats near cliff and plateau topography (Rodrick and Milner 1991). Grassland, oak savannah, alpine tundra, meadows, open woodland, and chaparral habitats provide suitable hunting habitat. With the increasing use of clearcutting in westside forests, many areas in western

Juvenile Golden Eagle gliding on a stiff breeze: white patches on wings and base of tail seen only in juveniles.

Washington are now providing suitable open habitat for Golden Eagles (Bruce et al. 1982).

Nesting. Golden Eagles construct their nests on cliff ledges and high rocky outcrops, in large mature or old-growth trees, on top of telephone poles, and on the ground (Bruce et al. 1982; Knight et al. 1982), but cliffs are generally used if

Golden Eagle adult feeding young on nest ledge.

available (Anderson and Bruce 1980). In western Washington, 20 of 21 nests were found in mature or old-growth Douglas-fir trees and the remaining nest was found on a cliff (Bruce et al. 1982). In British Columbia, 52 nests were mostly on cliff ledges (51%) or in trees (27%), with the remainder in overhanging rock faces, on top of rock bluffs and pinnacles, and caves (Campbell et al. 1990). Of the 14 tree nests, 9 were in Douglas-firs, 4 were in ponderosa pine, and one was in a snag. Most nests were lined with Douglas-fir boughs, grasses, bark, and mosses (Campbell et al. 1990).

Eggs and Young. The eggs are white or pale buffy, usually more or less spotted and blotched with brown (Godfrey 1986) and approximately 3.0 x 2.3 inches (76.2 x 58.4 mm) in size (Herron et al. 1985). Egg dates for 12 clutches ranged from 23 April to 11 June and clutch size ranged from 1 to 3 eggs, with 7 having 2 eggs (Campbell et al. 1990). Brood size for 42 broods ranged from 1 to 3 young, with 50% having 2

young (Campbell et al. 1990). Near Malheur NWR in Oregon, Thompson et al. (1982) recorded a 15-year average of 1.08 young fledged per territory, 1.7 young fledged per successful nest, and 51% of the nests were successful.

Hunting Behavior and Diet. The Golden Eagle hunts over open country for hares, rabbits, ground squirrels, marmots, snakes, birds, and sometimes new-born ungulates and carrion. In northeastern California and northwestern Nevada, black-tailed jackrabbits dominated the diet by frequency (76%), followed by Sage Grouse (17%), mountain cottontail (9%), yellow-bellied marmot (3%), Chukar (2%), and smaller numbers of 32 other prey species (Bloom and Hawks 1982). At Malheur NWR, a similar diet of black-tailed jackrabbit, cottontail, and marmot was found, but ducks were taken in place of game birds (Johnstone et al. 1982). Because Golden Eagles normally occupy open habitats, they also seem to have benefited from past clearcutting practices in heavily forested

View from a Golden Eagle nest ledge near Yakima Canyon, Washington.

regions where it was once too dense for them to inhabit (Bruce et al. 1982). In westside forests, Golden Eagles have been found to prey upon mountain beaver, snowshoe hare, and various birds (Bruce et al. 1982). Golden Eagles have favorite hunting perches on snags or rocks that are close to regular updrafts which allow them quick access to soaring height from which they can scan for prey (Johnsgard 1990). Capture may be made from high-speed glides from a soaring or perched position or while making low, flapping flights.

Territory and Density. Golden Eagles are territorial, but have extremely large home ranges which are impossible to defend efficiently. Nevertheless, there is a high regularity and stability in the spacing of pairs which are typically maintained annually, although pairs do not breed every year. Home range size in Utah for six pairs averaged 8.8 square miles (23 square km) (Smith and Murphy 1973). Knight et al. (1982) noted an average distance between nests (n=10) of 7.2 miles (11.5 km) along

View of Golden Eagle habitat and nest in large ponderosa pine near Yakima Canyon, Washington.

the Columbia River in north-central Washington.

Surveys. Helicopter surveys are the most efficient survey method because of the low nesting density of this species (Call 1978; Beecham and Kochert 1975). Road surveys are a cheaper alternative in areas with high road densities and good vantage points. Depending upon objectives, observers should make continuous observations while slowly driving (10-25 mph or 16-40 kmph) or point counts at periodic roadside stops (usually 0.5 mile apart or 0.8 km) (Kochert 1986) and scan the sky for several minutes at each stop. Where birds are detected, spotting scopes should be used to scan the area for possible nest sites and excrement trails (whitewash). Observers should try to maintain visual contact as long as possible because adult eagles will often lead you to their nest site. However, it pays to use a concealed position and camouflaged clothing because nesting Golden Eagles are often

Golden Eagle.

secretive and will not readily return to the nest if you are too conspicuous. If nests are not in view from roads, further ground and aerial surveys are needed to find the nest (Call 1978). Nests in forested areas are more difficult to find, and may occur in stands up to 1,640 feet (500 m) from the edge of open habitats and clearcuts (Bruce et al. 1982). Routes should be selected that are close to clearcuts, burns, and natural open areas such as rock outcrops, meadows, avalanche chutes, and large blow-downs. Preferably the routes should be located on or near upper slopes giving wide views, especially of ridgelines used for soaring.

Conservation and Management. There are no specific habitat management plans which have been previously proposed or used for the Golden Eagle. One habitat protection measure in forested regions is to protect existing nest sites by establishing no cut zones (e.g., 660 foot or 200 m radius) around active nests and would require closing the surrounding area (0.25 mile or 0.4

km radius around nest) to management from April 1 to August 15. Golden Eagles are sensitive to disturbance and nests built near roads are often unsuccessful (Call 1978). Recreational activities such as climbing or camping near cliffs should be avoided from 15 January to 15 July (Rodrick and Milner 1991). In western Washington, clearcutting can have beneficial effects for this species in areas that were formerly heavily forested (Bruce et al. 1982), but interspersion with mature and old-growth stands is recommended (Rodrick and Milner 1991). These clumps should be regularly spaced (<1 mile or 1.6 km apart) and located in higher elevation sites with steep slopes, alpine meadows, cliffs, rocky outcrops, and talus. Adjacent large areas of early seral stage forest (0-7 years) are suitable foraging areas for this species that mainly preys on hares, rabbits, and ground squirrels. Finally, designing power lines and power poles to prevent electrocution is also a valuable conservation measure for this open country raptor (Olendorff et al. 1981).

Golden Eagle lands on a road-killed deer.

STEVEN P. SACHS

AMERICAN KESTREL *(Falco sparverius)*
Length 8.5"; Wingspan 21"

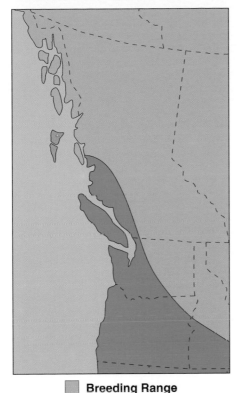

Breeding Range

Resident Range

American Kestrel adult female.

Range. This small falcon is locally common and widespread in preferred habitats throughout the Pacific Northwest. Kestrels most commonly breed at low to moderate elevations, but have been recorded at 5,000 to 6,000 feet (1,520 to 1,830 m) in Washington (Smith et al. 1997). The species quickly becomes rare to spotty in the mountains and northern British Columbia breeding from sea level to 5,800 feet (1,770 m) in elevation (Campbell et al. 1990). In Washington, a preference is shown for drier regions, and hence, they are virtually absent from the Olympic Peninsula and coast (Smith et al. 1997). In Oregon, it breeds widely throughout the state wherever open habitats occur (Csuti et al. 1997). This falcon is highly migratory, and winters from southern Canada into Washington and Oregon.

Status. Populations have been stable or possibly even increasing in recent times. Breeding Bird Survey routes on Pacific Northwest National Forests indicated a significant increase from 1968 to 1989, although statewide trends for Washington were not significant from 1980 to 1989 (Sharp 1992). Their current distribution is probably the same or greater than historical distribution owing to their great versatility in habitat use and use of man-made structures for nesting (Platt and Enderson 1989). Populations in Oregon and Washington were considered stable (Platt and Enderson 1989).

Habitat Requirements. American Kestrels prefer the comparatively open or partly open habitats of farmlands and fields interspersed with woodlands and small clumps of trees. They also occur along the edges of grassland and sagebrush communities provided that suitable food, roosting and nesting sites are available. In British Columbia, American Kestrels are most often found in open country and clearings such as open rangeland, grasslands, agricultural areas, and sagebrush areas, provided they are bordered by fences and other structures that are suitable for perch sites (Campbell et al. 1990). Habitats used during migration include almost any open area such as mountain burns, clearings, farmlands, parks, airports, and meadows (Campbell et al. 1990). Nest site habitats likewise include almost any open or semi-open areas where perch and roost sites and suitable food are available. If these are lacking the American Kestrel may nest and roost in urban and suburban open space, abandoned mills, and other industrial areas, and open woodlands. Old orchards, river corridors, tree-lined ravines and even tree-lined town and city roads may provide suitable nesting and roosting sites if sufficient open space in the form of

American Kestrels frequently perch on telephone wires, like this adult male.

cemeteries, playgrounds, and large lawns are available nearby for foraging purposes (Smith et al. 1997). Although generally found at lower elevations it will nest in parkland, meadows, burns, clear-cuts, and other open space at higher elevations providing nest sites and food supply are adequate (Smith et al. 1997).

Nesting. Nesting habitat requirements mainly center on the need for a cavity or other sheltered nest site (Knight et al. 1982). Apparently the female selects a nest site, choosing from natural cavities in trees, old woodpecker holes, niches and crevices in cliffs and rock ledges, or small openings in abandoned buildings or other structures. Of 261 nest sites in British Columbia, 73% were in cavities in live or dead trees, 23% in cavities in structures and most of the remainder were in cavities in cliffs (Campbell et al. 1990). Structures used included nest boxes (17% of total nests found), buildings, power poles and fence posts. Bird nests appropriated by nesting American Kestrels in British Columbia included nests of belted kingfisher, black-billed magpie, and American crow (Campbell et al. 1990). Nest heights of 166 tree nests in British Columbia varied from 3 to 90 feet (0.9 to 27.4 m) above ground. The actual nest itself is poorly constructed, typically little more than a scrape that is sometimes lined with feathers.

American Kestrel adult male.

Eggs and Young. The eggs are white or pinkish variably marked with browns (Godfrey 1986) and approximately 1.4 x 1.1 inches (35.6 x 27.9 mm) in size (Herron et al. 1985). Eggs are generally laid in late spring, typically from early April into June. Egg dates of 132 clutches in British Columbia ranged from 17 April to 20 July and clutch size for 104 clutches ranged from 1 to 6 eggs, with 77% having 4 or 5 eggs (Campbell et al. 1990). Brood size for 148 broods ranged from 1 to 6 young, with 51% having 3 or 4 young (Campbell et al. 1990). Dates for nests with young ranged from 14 May through 2 August but most young probably fledge by mid-summer (Campbell et al. 1990).

TOM BOSAKOWSKI

Juvenile American Kestrel perched on a wire.

Hunting Behavior and Diet. Throughout its range the Kestrel's diet consists mostly of small mammals, birds, and insects. Some birds and insects such as dragonflies are hunted on the wing, but others are taken by stoops from perches. Small mammals and ground-dwelling birds such as horned larks are often taken by hovering flights. In northern Utah, diet biomass for kestrels consisted of 38% mammals, 57% birds, and 2% insects (Smith and Murphy 1973). Hunting is done almost entirely from elevated perches with hovering, hawking flights, and foraging on foot making up less than 3% of all hunts (Balgooyen in Johnsgard 1990).

Territory and Density. These diminuitive falcons generally defend small territories during the breeding season. In northern Utah, Kestrels had home ranges averaging 168-200 acres (68 to 81 ha) in two years (Smith and Murphy 1973).

Survey Methods. This small falcon is very active in flight, but also has the habit of perching along roadways (powerlines, poles) and on other elevated perch sites (trees and snags) were it is easily detected. Surveys are conducted by driving available roads, searching clifflines, and systematically examining areas containing scattered tree stands for the presence of adult birds (Call 1978). Nests are typically located within a quarter to half-mile (0.4-0.8 km) of observed adults.

Conservation and Management. Protection of natural cavities in cliff faces and snags is an important management goal to provide adequate densities of suitable nesting structures. Where these sites are normally rare, erection of nest boxes is a practical way to improve conditions for nesting by Kestrels. Designs for making a Kestrel nest box are illustrated in Herron et al. (1985) and Call (1979) displays photographs of several other nest box designs that will work. In terms of foraging habitat, protection of native grasslands and prairies from excessive grazing, cultivation, and development is an important strategy to protect prey densities. American Kestrels are also at risk from environmental contaminants such as pesticides and herbicides. Henny et al. (1984) found that kestrel nesting success in Oregon declined when heptachlor levels in eggs increased above 1.5 ppm.

MERLIN *(Falco columbarius)*
Length 12"; Wingspan 23"

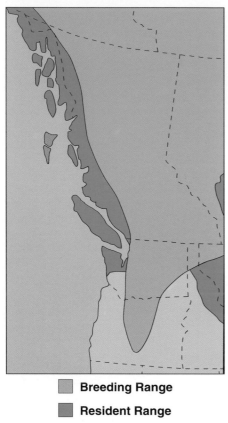

Breeding Range

Resident Range

Wintering Range

Range. The Washington GAP Analysis shows that the breeding range occurs on the westside of the Olympic Peninsula, the San Juan Islands, and one possible location in the southern Cascades (Smith et al. 1997). The northwest corner of Oregon and most forested regions of Washington (except Blue Mountains) are considered breeding and wintering range, albeit breeding is rare (Platt and Enderson 1989). In British Columbia, the entire province is considered breeding range, except for the Queen Charlotte Islands and the northern Mainland Coast (Godfrey 1986). It breeds on Vancouver Island, in Rivers Inlet, Fraser

A wintering Merlin (Taiga subspecies) north of Ocean Shores, Washington.

Lowlands, and east of the Coast Ranges in the Interior from sea level to 2,600 feet (790 m) in elevation (Campbell et al. 1990). The Merlin is highly migratory, and winters from southern Canada into Washington and Oregon.

Status. Because of its rarity as a breeding species in Washington and Oregon, the Merlin was found on only three Breeding Bird Survey routes from 1968 to 1989 including Wenatchee, Colville, and Mount Hood National Forests (Sharp 1992). The species is far more common in British Columbia. During the DDT-era, the *richardsonii* subspecies suffered population declines as a result of reproductive failure (mostly eggshell thinning) over most of its range and range contraction (Trimble 1975). Since the ban on DDT, Merlin numbers have climbed on Christmas Bird Counts (Johnsgard 1990). The Merlin is currently considered a state candidate species in Washington.

Habitat Requirements. Merlins breed primarily in the prairie-parkland ecotone, less commonly in riparian habitats, and rarely in juniper (Platt and Enderson 1989). Nesting habitat is in open to moderately dense woodland (deciduous or coniferous), forest openings, wooded prairie coulees (Godfrey 1986), deciduous shelterbelts (Fox 1964; Hodson 1976), and planted conifers in urban settings (Warkentin and James 1988). The Merlin hunts in a variety of habitats, especially outside the breeding season including coastlines, marshes, mudflats, open grasslands, woodlands, lakes, wetlands and early successional stages (Godfrey 1986).

Nesting. Merlins usually nest in an abandoned nest (crow or magpie) and occasionally in cavities of trees, cliffs, deserted buildings and on the ground (Trimble 1975; Ellis 1976; Godfrey 1986). Nest sites are usually adjacent to openings, forest edges, lakeshores, large rivers, bogs, cliffs, and on islands of large lakes (Trimble 1975). In British Columbia, 14 nests were found including: 13 in trees (Douglas-fir 4,

Juvenile Merlin close-up from north side of Grays Harbor, Washington.

Adult female Merlin (Pacific or Black subspecies).

spruces 4, pines 3, poplar 1, birch 1), and one on a cliff ledge (Campbell et al. 1990). Heights of 12 tree nests ranged from 20 to 150 feet (6.1 to 45.7 m) and the cliff nest was 13 feet (4 m) above ground.

Eggs and Young. The eggs are a creamy white ground color much hidden by profuse markings and blotches of brown (Godfrey 1986) and approximately 1.6 x 1.2 inches (40.6 x 30.5 mm) in size (Herron et al. 1985). Egg dates for 9 clutches ranged from 2 May to 6 July and clutch size for 10 clutches ranged from 1 to 4 eggs, with 7 having 2 or 3 eggs (Campbell et al. 1990). Brood size (n=27) ranged from 1 to 4 young, with 11 having 2 young (Campbell et al. 1990).

Hunting Behavior and Diet. The Merlin is adapted to feed primarily on small birds, but it occasionally takes small mammals and insects (Trimble 1975). Their food habits have been summarized worldwide as 80%

birds, 5% mammals, and 15% insects (Brown and Amadon 1968), although Bent (1937) included toads, lizards, and snakes. Smaller birds such as sparrows, larks, warblers, jays, and robins are usually taken (Trimble 1975), but larger birds such as rock dove, teal, and ptarmigan have been reported (Bent 1937). Hunting is accomplished mainly by three methods: low flight to surprise or flush prey, perch hunting (sit and wait), and high overflights with vertical diving.

Territory and Density. Because of their rarity in the region, Merlins nest at low densities. The closest nearest neighbor distance for nests was 10.6 miles (17 km) apart in Montana (Ellis 1976) while 3 pairs nested on a 3 mile (4.8 km) section of the North Saskatchewan River (Oliphant cited in Trimble 1975). Merlins consistently display vocal and aerial defense of their nest site as far as 0.9 mile (1.5 km) and frequently at a distance of 0.5 mile (0.8 km) (Trimble 1975).

Survey Methods. Boat surveys along rivers and lakes are an efficient method for locating Merlins nesting near water (Call 1978). At other inland sites, road surveys and systematic foot searches of suitable stands are probably the best methods. No data on broadcasting conspecific calls has been published for Merlins.

Conservation and Management. New Forestry and other conservative logging practices would probably reduce impacts to breeding Merlins, although a specific timber management plan for Merlins has not yet been developed to our knowledge. In addition, native grasslands and prairies need to be protected from excessive grazing, cultivation, and development (Trimble 1975). Continued and renewed use of chlorinated-hydrocarbon pesticides in Central and South America could increase contamination levels of migratory birds taken as prey by Merlins (Platt and Enderson 1989).

Adult male Merlin (Pacific or Black subspecies).

GYRFALCON *(Falco rusticolus)*
Length 20"; Wingspan 48"

Gyrfalcon (gray morph).

Resident Range

— **Southern Limit of Regular Occurrence**

Range. In British Columbia, the Gyrfalcon is an uncommon summer breeding species in the extreme northwest, and a rare winter visitor to southeastern Vancouver Island and the Fraser Lowlands, casual in the northern interior, and very rare in the central-southern interior. This large falcon nests in British Columbia throughout the Northern Mountains and Plateaus region (Campbell et al. 1990). A band recovery showed that Gyrfalcons wintering in southwestern British Columbia were from nests located in the south Yukon (Campbell et al. 1990). In Washington and Oregon, the Gyrfalcon is a rare winter visitor. Watson et al. (1989) listed 7 occurrences of the Gyrfalcon in Oregon, of

which 6 were in February and March and one in September; the majority of sightings were in open habitats along the coast. Three different color morphs are known from British Columbia; 69% gray, 27% dark, and 4% white (Campbell et al. 1990).

Status. There is no evidence of long-term population change in North America (Clum and Cade 1994). Most Gyrfalcons taken for falconry are from captive-breeding, although immatures are still legally harvested in several states and provinces (Clum and Cade 1994). Currently, it is Blue-Listed in British Columbia.

Habitat Requirements. The Gyrfalcon is a bird of open and semi-open landscapes and is most often associated with arctic and alpine tundra along rivers and seacoasts (Clum and Cade 1994). In British Columbia, the Gyrfalcon is most often associated with open and semi-open habitats, from coastal shores to alpine meadows and typically breeds in tundra and taiga habitats at elevations of 3,940 to 5,700 feet (1,200 to 1,740 m) (Campbell et al. 1990). Gyrfalcon habitat requirements in winter also include open habitats and an adequate food supply. They frequently winter along the coast in coastal habitats, especially along salt marshes, sandy and rocky beaches, and coastal clifflines and seamounts from British Columbia southward through Oregon, although it becomes much rarer as a wintering bird in Oregon. In the Puget Sound lowlands it is more often found in extensive river deltas.

Nesting. Nests are built on rocky outcrops, cliffs, ledges, river bluffs surrounded by tundra, and in open coniferous forests where an old stick nest of a raven, crow, or raptor may also be appropriated (Campbell et al. 1990). Eggs are laid in a shallow scrape on a ledge or cliff line. Nest sites were located on ledges and in unused Golden Eagle nests and all nests were at least partly protected by overhanging ledges (Campbell et al. 1990). Prey abundance influences its breeding behavior and distribution, and during years when ptarmigan populations are low, Gyrfalcons will not nest and may abandon their territory and wander southwards.

Eggs and Young. The eggs are yellowish and measure an average of 2.3 x 1.8 inches

(59.4 x 45.3 mm) in size (Bent 1938). Clutches generally average 4 eggs but may range from 3-5 eggs. Information on Gyrfalcon nesting in British Columbia suggest that eggs are laid in April and young are in the nest from May-June through mid-July and 12 broods ranged from 2-5 young (Campbell et al. 1990).

Hunting Behavior and Diet. Ptarmigan are a staple food item but other prey may include waterfowl, shorebirds, seabirds, and grouse. In British Columbia, its breeding distribution is associated with open areas where ptarmigan are common (Campbell et al. 1990) while in winter it occurs in habitats with ample waterfowl, shorebirds, gulls, and other waterbirds that comprise its opportunistic predation. The Gyrfalcon hunts from perches or by quartering low, back and forth over the tundra, coastal salt marsh, or other suitable open habitat. Clum and Cade (1994) summarized its main methods of finding food as (1) hunting from perches on a rock or mound that offers a commanding view of the terrain (2) quartering about terrain in search of prey and (3) soaring along ridges and valleys. Most prey

DAVID H. ELLIS

Gyrfalcon (dark morph).

Gyrfalcon (white morph).

is chased and then captured in powerful dives or stoops (Clum and Cade 1994).

Territory and Density Nesting territories center on the cliff site where the nest is located and the actual area defended usually describes an oval about 0.9 miles (1,400 m) long and 1,312-1,642 feet (400-500 m) deep (Platt 1977). White and Nelson (1991) observed that a female with older nestlings remained within 2 miles (3.2 km) of the nest while the male patrolled a huge 77 square mile (200 square km) area. Density of territories varies widely depending on availability of nest sites and food, but recorded mean internest distance ranges 3.1 to 58 miles (5 to 93 km) (Clum and Cade 1994). Territories are advertised by fly-by displays including eyrie fly-by by the male, who flies parallel to the cliff face in a broad figure eight pattern. Territorial defense against intruders may involve active pursuit and aggressive vocalizations when needed (Clum and Cade 1994). The Gyrfalcon will also defend territories against other birds of prey including the Northern Harrier, Peregrine Falcon, Rough-legged Hawk, Golden Eagle, and Red-tailed Hawk as well as other predators such as Common Raven, Red Fox, and Wolverine (Clum and Cade 1994).

Surveys. Ground, aerial, or boat surveys should be conducted in April or May (Call 1978). Helicopter surveys are the most desirable, because of poor access into most nesting areas. A Heliocarrier with tundra tires has also been used for surveys. Nest sites and roost sites of Gyrfalcons can often be located by the excrement (whitewash) that streams down the cliff, ledge, or rock outcrop that marks their nest or favorite perch and roost sites. In mid-June, re-checks of nest sites for nesting success can be done from a Super Cub, by making several passes (Call 1978).

Conservation and Management. Due to the extreme remoteness of their nesting habitat, no specific efforts have been undertaken to conserve habitat or manage nest sites for this species The only management has been related to offsetting falconry take, such as changing harvest regulations, export/import laws, and captive breeding programs (Clum and Cade 1994).

PEREGRINE FALCON (*Falco peregrinus*)
Length 15"; Wingspan 40"

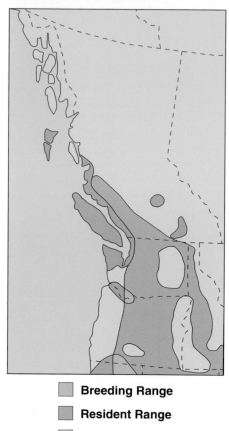

Adult female Peregrine Falcon
(Peale's subspecies).

■ **Breeding Range**

■ **Resident Range**

☐ **Wintering Range**

Range. The breeding range in Washington occurs along Puget Sound, The San Juan Islands, Northern Coast, with the only interior breeding sites on the Columbia River and Hells Canyon in the southeastern tip of the state (Smith et al. 1997). However, unpublished data from Washington Department of Fish and Wildlife also indicate at least 7 eyries in the Cascades. In Oregon, breeding is mostly limited to the Columbia River Gorge and southwestern corner of the state along the California border (Platt and Enderson 1989). In British Columbia, the entire province is considered breeding range by Godfrey (1986).

Wintering range is limited primarily to the coastline and Coast Mountains in Oregon and Washington (Platt and Enderson 1989). In British Columbia, most nesting is known from along coastal regions including the Fraser Lowlands, southern Gulf Islands in the Strait of Georgia, northwestern Vancouver Island, islands off the central main coast, and the Queen Charlotte Islands (Campbell et al. 1990). Some fall migration movement may occur in the northern part of the range, including Washington, and some adults remain near the nest site year-round but range more widely during winter. Some falcons may winter in city landscapes.

In the Pacific Northwest, three subspecies occur, they are the *anatum, pealei,* and *tundrius* (Allen 1991, Campbell et al. 1990). The *pealei* subspecies has a primarily coastal breeding distribution in Washington and the *anatum* subspecies has a primarily inland distrbution except in the San Juan Islands (Hayes and Buchanan 2001). Campbell et al. (1990) considers the pealei subspecies as a marine Peregrine, essentially a resident of islands and headlands of the Pacific Coast in British Columbia. The *tundrius* subspecies breeds on the arctic tundra, and is generally considered a migrant in the Pacific Northwest, although it may be an extremely rare winter resident.

Status. The Peregrine Falcon was formerly a more common breeding bird throughout the Pacific Northwest. Breeding populations were considered stable prior to World War II, but worldwide reproductive failures and population declines were first recognized in the 1950s (Hickey and Anderson 1969). In Oregon, populations declined gradually in the 1930s and 40s, but the majority of nests were abandoned in the 1950s, although a few nests were still occupied through the 1970s (Henny and Nelson 1981). Factors suspected of contributing to peregrine falcon population declines included human disturbance,

shooting, and habitat loss. However, the primary factor that led to the more dramatic declines in peregrine falcon populations was the environmental contamination of the food chain resulting from the introduction of DDT as an agricultural pesticide, which led to eggshell thinning and nesting failure (Hickey and Anderson 1968). In 1970, the American peregrine (*F. p. anatum*) was placed on the Federal endangered species list (U.S. Fish and Wildlife Service 1982).

The objective of the Pacific Coast Recovery Plan was to re-establish 30 pairs of Peregrines in Washington, 30 pairs in Oregon, 120 pairs in California, and 5 pairs in Nevada with an average productivity of 1.5 young per active territory, over a 5-year period to achieve delisting (U.S. Fish and Wildlife Service 1982). Since the late 70's, Peregrine populations have shown a continuing trend of recovery. Coastal populations in Washington have increased dramatically from 3 to 24 pairs and an average of 1.5 to 3.0 young are now produced per successful nest (Wilson et al. 2000). In Washington state, there were only 4 known breeding

Juvenile Peregrine Falcon banded as a nestling in the San Jaun Islands (6/2/2001) of Washington by Bud Anderson of the Falcon Research Group and captured by Daniel E. Varland on the Long Beach Peninsula (9/22/2001).

pairs in 1980 compared to 56 pairs in 2000 (Hayes and Buchanan 2001). In light of their rapid recovery, federal de-listing was recently proposed (Cade et al. 1997) and occurred in August of 1999 (Federal Register 1999), although some researchers believe the decision is premature (Pagel et al. 1996; Pagel and Bell 1997). Federal delisting of a species does not require its removal from state endangered and threatened species lists. The Peregrine remains on the state endangered list in Washington, and still can not be taken from the wild for falconry purposes (Hayes and Buchanan 2001). The *anatum* and *tundrius* subspecies are currently listed as endangered in Oregon. In British Columbia, the *anatum* subspecies is Red-Listed and the *pealei* and *tundrius* subspecies are Blue-Listed.

Habitat Requirements. Primary nesting habitat for this large falcon includes cliffs with ledges or small caves for nesting and roosting, and a source of water in conjunction with an adequate prey base of small to medium-sized birds (U.S. Fish and Wildlife Service 1982; Johnsgard 1990). Nest sites are selected where cliffs occur in conjunction with forest, grassland, beach or shoreline habitat (Sharp 1992). Most nest sites in Washington were found within 200 feet of a source of freshwater, either a creek or waterbody greater than 3 acres, and nest sites have occurred up to 5,500 feet (1,676 m) in elevation (Hayes and Buchanan 2001). Suitable foraging habitat exists along beaches, bays, and estuaries along the coast where shorebirds, waterfowl, and other migratory birds congregate. Intertidal flats, estuaries, and inland wetland habitats may become more important in winter such as the Skagit Flats, Grays Harbor, and Willapa Bay in Washington (U.S. Fish and Wildlife Service 1982).

Nesting. Peregrine Falcon nesting occurs primarily on sheer cliffs, ledges and rocky outcrops ranging in height from 75 to 2,000 feet (23 to 600 m) (Hickey 1969; Cade 1982; Cade et al. 1988), but occasionally they nest in snags, eagle nests, talus slopes, cutbanks, pinnacles, sand dunes, buildings, and bridges (Sharp 1992). Nest sites usually provide a panoramic view of open country, often overlook water, and are always associated with an abundance of passerine, waterfowl, or shorebird prey (Johnsgard 1990). In British Columbia, 93% of 305 coastal nests were situated on ledges of rocky cliffs and remaining nests were on grassy benches of rocky bluffs (11), and abandoned bird nests, including Pelagic Cormorant (6), Bald

An adult Peregrine Falcon soaring.

FRANK SCHLEICHER

Eagle (4), and Common Raven (1) (Campbell et al. 1990). Heights of 64 cliff nests ranged from 15 to 1,100 feet (4.6 to 335 m), with 50% recorded between 40 to 80 feet (12 and 24 m) (Campbell et al. 1990).

Eggs and Young. The eggs are a creamy ground color concealed by heavy markings of rich reddish-browns (Godfrey 1986) and approximately 2.2 x 1.7 inches (55.9 x 43.2 mm) in size (Herron et al. 1985). Egg dates of 155 coastal clutches in British Columbia ranged from 20 April to 7 May and clutch size for 149 clutches ranged from 1 to 5 eggs, with 74% having 3 or 4 eggs (Campbell et al. 1990). Brood size for 247 broods ranged from 1 to 5 young, with 76% having 2 or 3 young (Campbell et al. 1990).

Hunting Behavior and Diet. Nesting Peregrines forage over a large area, which frequently includes bodies of water, marshes, shorelines, wooded areas adjacent to water, and grasslands (U.S. Fish and Wildlife Service 1982). The Peregrine preys on birds that range in size from small passerines to waterfowl (as large as geese). Columbiform birds (doves and pigeons) are preferred prey wherever they occur within the Peregrine's range (Cade 1982). In a study of wintering Peregrines near Sequim, Washington, 27 percent of the kills and 44 percent of the hunts were waterfowl, 42 percent of the kills and 26 percent of the hunts were passerine, and 3 percent of the kills were Mew Gulls (Dobler 1993). Foraging habitat can be characterized as an area with sufficient abundance of prey and physiographic features and foliage profiles that result in prey being vulnerable to Peregrine attacks (Hunt 1988). Winter food is waterfowl, shorebirds and passerines, and conifer snags are sometimes common perch sites (U.S. Fish and Wildlife Service 1982; Dobler 1993; Dekker 1995). Their preference for open country such as marshes, coastal rivers, shorelines, estuaries, and farmland allows them to ascend and drop on their prey from heights of 50 meters (150'), at speeds

A juvenile Peregrine Falcon leaps into the air.

FRANK SCHLEICHER

of 288 kmph (180 mph) (Johnsgard 1990). Prey are either struck dead from vertical stoops and are recovered on the ground or they are seized in flight (Johnsgard 1990). Peregrines may also still-hunt from a perch (Cade 1982), and occasionally they may employ "solitary flushing" of ground-dwelling birds or aerial "hawking" of insects (Johnsgard 1990). Peregrines often use aerial "waiting on" which involves searching for prey while circling or soaring high (Cade 1982), especially while waiting for seabirds to return to their nesting cliffs (Beebe 1960). When hunting on the ocean, Peregrines will sometimes conceal their approach behind waves by flying fast and low to surprise surface floating waterbirds, which panic and either dive or attempt to fly (Cade 1982, Dekker and Bogaert 1997).

Territory and Density. In good habitat, pairs can nest fairly close together, although individuals can hunt at great distances from the nest. At least 50 to 75 pairs breed on the Queen Charlotte Islands, the highest concentration in British Columbia (Campbell et al. 1990). In a dense island population on the British Columbia coast, Beebe (1960) found the average distance between pairs was about 1 mile (1.6 km). In Alaska, Cade (1960) found the minimum nearest neighbor distance between nests was 0.25 miles (0.4 km) apart and Peregrines attacked intruders up to 0.6 to 1.0 mile (900 to 1600 m) from their nest. In Utah, the Peregrine has hunted as far as 19 miles (30 km) from its nest (Sharp 1992).

Survey Methods. Aerial surveys are the most practical method when great distances and thousand of miles of streams are involved (Call 1978). If a helicopter is flown slowly across a cliff face, whitewash can be observed and adults may be observed as they flush. Without air support, float trips and ground surveys (by vehicle or foot) can be used to examine better habitats with binoculars and spotting scopes. When possible, the top of the cliff should be walked, but at least five hours should be spent before a cliff is considered unoccupied. Surveyors should minimize disturbance during egg-laying and incubation in April. Usually after June 1, the young are big enough to withstand chills, if the parents flush.

Conservation and Management.
Following the ban on DDT, Peregrine populations have rebounded or have been nursed back to health, partly with programmatic artificial management geared to increase their productivity. These methods include egg manipulation, captive breeding/hacking, double clutching, augmentation (adding chicks or eggs), fostering, and cross-fostering activities (U.S. Fish and Wildlife Service 1982). Some cliffs formerly used by Peregrine Falcons have been abandoned following new housing developments (at the top and bottom of cliffs) and recreational activities (U.S. Fish and Wildlife Service 1982). In addition, loss of foraging areas at marshes, savannahs, and shorelines has occurred with increased urbanization. Protection of cliff nest sites and adjacent foraging habitat should be a top priority for preserving these incredible falcons, but is often difficult because of private land ownership in shoreline communities. Dobler (1993) noted that 89% of the Washington coastline was in private ownership. Wilson et al. (2000) suggested that close monitoring should continue until populations have stabilized.

Adult female Peregrine Falcon (Peale's subspecies) at Ocean Shores, Washington.

PRAIRIE FALCON *(Falco mexicanus)*
Length 16"; Wingspan 40"

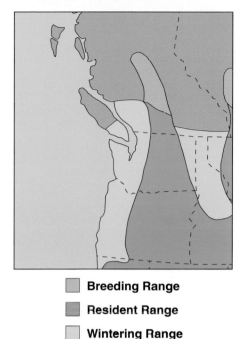

■ **Breeding Range**

■ **Resident Range**

■ **Wintering Range**

Adult Prairie Falcon.

Range. This large falcon is generally restricted to open habitats of the western North America. In the Pacific Northwest, the range of the Prairie Falcon extends from the palouse prairies and shrub steppe of eastern Oregon northward through eastern Washington and into south-central British Columbia. In British Columbia, they nest between 1,475 to 2,950 feet (450 and 900 m) in elevation (Campbell et al. 1990). Prairie falcons are more common across the Pacific Northwest in autumn, as migrants augment local populations of permanent residents. Numbers drop in winter, but a few hardy individuals occur within the southern and eastern portion of the falcon's range in Washington and Oregon. Post-breeding dispersal may lead some birds to very high elevations such as late-summer birds observed high on Mount Rainier and Slate Peak in Washington (Smith et al. 1997).

Status. In a regional review, most western states judged the Prairie Falcon populations to be stable or unknown, although California did not submit data (Platt and Enderson 1989). Migration trends from 1977 to 1991 showed a nonsignificant change at autumn hawk watches in Utah, Nevada, and New Mexico (Hoffmann et al. 1992). In past years, this falcon has suffered declines in nesting productivity that were linked with mercury poisoning, and also eggshell thinning from pesticides. Both conservation problems probably arise because of their high use of Horned Larks and other gramnivores as a staple food base throughout much of their western range (Ehrlich et al. 1988). Campbell et al. (1990) noted declines in the Okanagan region of southern British Columbia and linked these declines with direct human interference at active nest sites and increasing use of pesticides, but also noted that weather and other factors may influence the numbers of this species at its extreme northern range. Currently, this falcon is Red-Listed in British Columbia.

Habitat. Prairie Falcons are open-country birds that typically nest, forage, and winter in shrub-steppe grasslands and semiarid desert habitat (Steenhof 1998). Smith et al. (1997) noted that forest openings are also good prairie falcon habitat, but ponderosa pine and Douglas-fir were peripheral and other types were not used. Nest-site habitat includes foothills, river valleys, canyons and rock outcrops, or any habitat that provides a combination of steep escarpments, cliffs, and ledges for nesting and nearby open or semi-open country for foraging. Marginal cliff and rock outcrop sites are sometimes selected near agricultural and riparian areas if a suitable prey base is available. Nonbreeding falcons occur in a wide variety of open country habitats ranging from alpine meadows to grasslands and desert brush, but agricultural landscapes and marshy areas are less used. Littlefield (1990) noted that Prairie Falcons in the Malheur NWR of southeastern Oregon preferred mudflats, agricultural areas, and sagebrush uplands for feeding areas and nested in rimrock country. In winter, the species is also found on farmland, lakes, and reservoirs, but is usually scarce along the immediate coast.

Nesting. The Prairie Falcon usually nests on sheltered ledges overlooking large, open expanses. Cliff ledges, crevices in large rock outcrops, rimrocks, old quarries, and mountain cliff lines are the preferred nesting sites. Nest sites are usually located in sheer or nearly sheer walls and may range anywhere from 20 to 400 feet (7 to 120 m) high (Johnsgard 1990). In British Columbia, all 12 known nests were located on cliffs with 8 on ledges, 2 in caves, 1 in a crevice, and 1 in a pothole, and nesting cliffs ranged in height from 50 to 450 feet (15 to 138 m) (Campbell et al. 1990). All nest sites had protective overhangs that provided shade and shelter. The Prairie Falcon does not

make a nest, but instead scrapes loose debris to form a small depression ("nest scrape") to hold eggs (Steenhof 1998). Nests typically consist of unadorned substrates although some may be decorated with a few twigs of greenery or scraps of wood and other debris.

Eggs and Young. The eggs vary in color from creamy white to pink or russet; usually speckled, spotted, and clouded with brown, cinnamon, or rufous (Steenhof 1998) and are approximately 2.1 x 1.6 inches (53.3 x 40.6 mm) in size (Herron et al. 1985). In Malheur NWR of southeastern Oregon, a small influx of falcons occurred between mid-March and mid-April and nesting began almost immediately with the earliest clutches found 27 March and young usually fledging between June and early July (Littlefield 1990). Campbell et al. (1990) suggested that in British Columbia most clutches were laid in late March or April and broods were found in the nest from 27 April to 5 August although most were found during the first two weeks of July. Clutch size for 3 clutches in British Columbia ranged from 3 to 4 eggs and brood size for 8 broods ranged from 1 to 5 young, with 4 broods having 3 or 4 young (Campbell et al. 1990).

Hunting Behavior and Diet. Staple prey include small to medium-sized birds,

Adult female Prairie Falcon in flight.

Prairie Falcon.

mammals, and occasionally lizards, but especially horned larks (Steenhof 1998). Smith et al. (1997) noted that favored prey in Washington included ground squirrels, rabbits, California Quail, Chukar, Gray Partridge and other upland game birds. Prairie falcons generally hunt from a perch, soaring, or in low-level on-the-wing power flights (Phipps 1979). Prairie Falcons typically pursue prey in a swift, direct flight that ends with a low-angled stoop (White 1962). Both males and females cache excess food in separate caches (Steenhof 1998). Breeding adults may travel as much as 16 miles from their nest to find prey (Johnsgard 1990).

Territories and Density. The actual size of the defended territory is typically small and centered around the nest site, but adults forage over huge undefended home ranges throughout the nesting season (Steenhof 1998). Across western North America, breeding season home ranges averaged from 23 to 120 square miles (59 to 315 square km) (Steenhof 1998). Average distances between active nests in northern Montana was 0.60 miles (0.98 km), but nearest neighbor distances were much lower in areas that had a high density of breeding falcons such as the Snake River in Idaho (Steenhof 1998). Territories are selected and claimed by males, usually by aerial displays high within the territory. These displays also serve to attract females which are courted

by spectacular aerial flights of parabolas, calling, and strutting back and forth along a ledge or above a cliff crevice that can serve as a suitable nest site. As courtship continues, the female may accompany the male on his territorial advertisement and courtship flights (Steenhof 1998). If disturbed early in the breeding season this shy falcon will abandon its nest and often its territory and move elsewhere.

Survey Methods. These falcons can be surveyed from the ground, boat, or air by observing cliff faces for the presence of whitewash (Call 1978), and of course, by following adult birds in flight as they bring prey back to their nest (DGS). Parent birds are extremely vocal when an intruder approaches a nest containing young and will often make terrific stoops to within a few feet of an intruder's head (Call 1978). In addition to breeding populations, migration counts provide information on local and regional status of this falcon.

Conservation and Management. Steenhof (1998) recognized four general management strategies that could help Prairie Falcons, including: (1) improving nest site availability with artificial nest structures, (2) managing habitat for prey populations, (3) providing protection from human disturbance with nest buffers, and (4) restoring populations through captive breeding, hacking, and egg manipulations. This falcon is sometimes precluded from otherwise favorable habitat within its range by lack of suitable natural nesting sites (Smith et al. 1997). A limited management aim of nesting platforms has met with some success (Littlefield 1990) and wider use of artificial nest platforms in open and semi-open habitats might help population recovery efforts. Various distances have been proposed for disturbance buffers (range = 1,312 to 3,280 feet or 400 to 1,000 m), but one study demonstrated that a buffer of 410 feet (125 m) was effective in reducing disturbance from blasting activity (Holthuijzen et al. 1990).

BARN OWL *(Tyto alba)*
Length 14"; Wingspan 44"

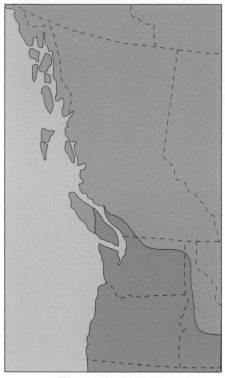

Barn Owl.

Resident Range

Range. The Barn Owl is the most wide-spread owl in the world, found on all continents except for Antarctica. The Barn Owl is considered an uncommon permanent resident that occurs locally over parts of the Pacific Northwest from Oregon in the south through southern British Columbia. In Oregon, the Barn Owl breeds mainly east of the Cascades in arid, open country, but also in the Willamette Valley and sporadically throughout the Coast and Cascade Ranges (Csuti et al. 1997). In Washington, Barn Owls are uncommon residents along the southern border of the state. They also extend in a narrow coastal band from the Columbia River and the Canadian boundary and east to Walla Walla (Jewett et al. 1953).

Individuals and pairs are essentially nonmigratory and the winter range is the same as at other times of the year. However, northerly populations may migrate, especially during harsher winters (Marti 1992).

Status. There is little information known about the population status of this nocturnal owl within this range, although it does appear to be stable. There is some evidence that Barn Owls have recently expanded their distribution into northwestern Washington and southern British Columbia (Marti and Marks 1989). Continental-wide declines in numbers of Barn Owls caused them to be included on the Blue List from 1972-81 and listed as a Species of Special Concern from 1982-86 (Tate and Tate 1982; Ehrlich et al. 1988). Throughout their range, population declines have been linked primarily to habitat loss, especially loss of farmland, pastures, and natural grasslands brought about by increasing urbanization (Colvin et al. 1984; Colvin 1985; Marti 1992). The Barn Owl remains Blue-Listed in British Columbia.

Habitat Requirements. The Barn Owl is most commonly found in open habitats, semiarid grasslands, deserts, open woodlands, and the mosaic of woodland and edge habitats that occurs in open space of cities and suburbs. Perhaps the most tolerant or at least the most adaptable of all raptors, they can be exceptionally abundant in farming regions where old barns provide nest sites, while the rats and mice of farms and fields provide a staple food base (Gabrielson and Jewett 1970; Marti 1992).

Nesting. Barn Owls are equally adaptable in choice of nest sites and almost any dark, elevated cavity can serve as a nest site. In natural habitats, they select nest sites on cliffs with crevices, caves, bankside cavities, and large cavities in trees and snags (DGS; Marti 1992). In man-made structures,

nests have been found in barn lofts, old buildings, silos, pipes, old smokestacks, church steeples, haystacks, nest boxes, sheltered pilings and pier structures (Call 1978; Marti 1992). In British Columbia, 93% of 221 nests were situated in man-made structures and nest heights for all nests ranged from 4 to 112 feet (1.2 to 34.2 m) above ground (Campbell et al. 1990). No nest is constructed, but the female may rearrange substrate materials including pellet fragments into a shallow bowl for the eggs (DGS). In the Pacific Northwest, these owls typically nest from late February or March into June but they are capable of nesting in almost every month of the year (Marti 1992). Nesting dates from Oregon are April 20 and April 24, 1924 (Gabrielson and Jewett 1970).

Eggs and Young. The eggs are white (Godfrey 1986) and average about 1.7 x 1.3 inches (43.2 x 33.0 mm) in size (Herron et al. 1985). Incubation duties are performed mostly by the female although occasionally males can be observed sitting side-by-side

Barn Owlets in cave nest from Benton County, eastern Washington.

with the females on the nest, although whether he is helping to incubate the eggs is unknown (DGS). Egg dates for British Columbia have been recorded for every month of the year, but most (74%) occurred between 7 March and 3 May (Campbell et al. 1990). Barn Owls often lay large clutches, averaging 5-6 eggs but ranging from 2-12 eggs (Marti 1992). Clutch size for 84 clutches in British Columbia ranged from 1 to 12 eggs, with 54% having 3 or 4 eggs, and brood size for 154 broods ranged from 1 to 9 young, with 63% of broods having 3 to 5 young (Campbell et al. 1990).

Hunting Behavior and Diet. While voles and mice comprise their main prey, Barn Owls are sufficiently opportunistic to take a wide variety of prey when available, ranging from fish, amphibians, lizards, snakes, and birds, and an assortment of invertebrates such as earthworms (DGS; Marti 1992). A study of 10 pairs of Barn Owls in northeastern Oregon revealed that voles were the most frequent prey items (1,620 of 2,513) in over 825 pellets examined (Bull

and Akenson 1984). Deer mice and pocket gophers (*Thomomys talpoides*) were the next most important prey items, but shrews, house mice, and birds made up less than 10% of the diet. Barn Owls are renowned hunters and are considered especially good "ratters" readily taking Norway rats and black rats. For this reason they have frequently been transplanted to inner cities to help control rodent populations. Enlightened farmers also encourage nesting by Barn Owls as they help keep mouse and vole populations in check around the farmyards and pastures (Gabrielson and Jewett 1970). Hunting begins in the twilight hours of dusk and continues all through the night, depending on the number of nestlings they have to feed. They are possibly the most efficient of all owls in hunting, and a number of scientific experiments have shown that this owl can find food even in total darkness, relying only on their exceptional hearing to find prey. Barn Owls hunt by making extended flapping flights, coursing low over open terrain, and sometimes by hovering in place.

Barn Owl perched on a telephone wire along a road.

Barn Owl portrait.

JEAN-LUC CARTRON

Territory and Density. Local density of nesting Barn Owls usually hinges on food abundance as well as the availability of nesting and roosting sites (DGS; Marti 1992). They can be locally abundant, occurring in close proximity, often in loose colonies of several breeding pairs given optimum conditions (Smith et al. 1974). Home ranges can be large, although few data are available for the Northwest. In New Jersey, home ranges averaged 1,771 acres (717 ha) and maximum distance from roost to hunting area was 3.5 miles (5.6 km) (Hegdal and Blaskiewicz 1984).

Survey Methods. Barn Owls are most frequently found by searching old buildings, barns, silos, or other man-made structures, but cavities in claybanks, large snags and trees, and cliffs should also be checked (Call 1978).

Conservation and Management. Given adequate conditions, Barn Owls exhibit a high reproductive rate characteristic of an r-selected life history strategy (Colvin et al. 1984; Marti 1997), hence they can respond well to selected conservation and management strategies. Conservation strategies have focused on captive-breeding (Maestrelli 1973), nest box programs, and release of captive-bred Barn Owls in several states to establish breeding pairs. However, the survival and productivity results from these efforts have been mixed. Lack of good population recoveries has been linked with inadequate prey populations and foraging habitat (Colvin 1985; Marti 1988).

FLAMMULATED OWL *(Otus flammeolus)*
Length 6"; Wingspan 14"

Breeding Range

Range. The Flammulated Owl is mostly confined to the higher elevations of the western United States and Canada (Ehrlich et al. 1988). In the Pacific Northwest, the

Flammulated Owl breeds locally from southern British Columbia south through eastern Washington and Oregon (Marshall 1992a). Breeding is rare in British Columbia, where they breed locally in the Thompson-Okanagan Plateau region at elevations from 2,000 to 3,970 feet (610 to 1,210 m) (Campbell et al. 1990). In Washington, they occur in the mid-slope forests of the Blue Mountains and in the Cascades of southeastern Washington (Smith et al. 1997). In Oregon, its breeding distribution closely follows the zone of ponderosa pine forests on the eastslope of the Cascade Range, Klammath Mountains, and Blue Mountains (Csuti et al. 1997). This neotropical migrant is highly migratory and in winter the northern birds move southward, wintering either in the southern United States or down through the highlands of Mexico and into Guatemala and El Salvador.

Flammulated Owl.

Status. The status of this little-known owl is unknown, but there is no evidence of population changes in the Pacific Northwest (McCallum 1994a). In Oregon, this small owl has long been considered an extremely rare resident of the eastern part of the state (Gabrielson and Jewett 1970). It is currently included as a sensitive species for the state and the U.S. Forest Service (Verner 1994), partly because little is known of its distribution and ecology. In Washington, this owl is uncommon and local in mature coniferous forests in eastern Washington (Smith et al. 1997). In British Columbia, centers of abundance were all in the southern portion of the province and include the Okanagan Valley, the South Thompson River Valley, and the southerly Rocky Mountain trench (Howie and Ritcey 1987). This owl is currently Blue-Listed in British Columbia.

Habitat Requirements. The Flammulated Owl is most commonly associated with mature and old growth montane coniferous forests, especially forests of ponderosa pine, and grand fir/Douglas-fir forests with relatively open canopies (Goggans 1985; Rodrick and Milner 1991). Mixed pine and oak woodlands may also be used for roosting and breeding. In eastern Washington breeding pairs were found in stands of mature ponderosa pine and Douglas-fir although many available stands were not used (Smith et al. 1997). Breeding habitat in British Columbia is represented by well-spaced Douglas firs and ponderosa pine, giving a park-like appearance with a very open understory of pinegrass, bluebunch wheatgrass, birch-leafed spirea, and isolated larger shrubs such as saskatoon (Campbell et al. 1990). In British Columbia, Flammulated Owls were found associated with interior Douglas-fir habitats (Howie and Ritcey 1987), especially the very dry submontane interior zone of the Douglas-fir zone (Mitchell and Green 1981) and no birds were found in the ponderosa pine zone. Howie and Ritcey (1987)

noted that near Kamloops, most owls were found in mature and old-growth (100-200 years) Douglas-fir stands, whereas in the Wheeler Mountain area, records were from 140-250-year-old stands of large Douglas-fir mixed with ponderosa pine, with 35-65 percent canopy closure and at least two canopy layers. Flammulated Owls were absent from clearcut areas and younger forests less than 80 years old. Most core areas were located near clearings or areas of brushy cover (Bull and Anderson 1978).

Nesting. Nests are generally located in natural tree cavities or in abandoned woodpecker holes. In British Columbia, most nests (10 of 16) were in old woodpecker holes in dead Douglas firs and ponderosa pine snags, and the remaining 6 were in nest boxes, and nest heights ranged from 5 to 44 feet (1.5 to 13.4 m) above ground (Campbell et al. 1990). In northeastern Oregon, these owls used a higher proportion of Pileated Woodpecker holes than expected based on availablity (Bull et al. 1990). Average nest tree diameter was 28 inches (72 cm), average nest height was 39.4 feet (12 m), and nest trees were found more often than expected on ridges and upper slopes (Bull et al. 1990). In Washington, nest sites were found in cavities or in holes about 7 to 40 feet (2 to 12 m) high that had been excavated by other birds (Rodrick and Milner 1991). Nest sites were in live trees or snags at least 12 inches (30 cm) in diameter or greater (Rodrick and Milner 1991). Flammulated Owls may rarely use nest boxes for breeding (Bloom 1983). Cannings and Cannings (1982) reported a pair of Flammulated Owls breeding in a nest box located in the Okanagan Valley of British Columbia. Bent (1938) reported that the peak nesting activity for this owl was from mid-June to mid-July. The nest proper consists of a shallow scrape at the bottom of the tree cavity, occasionally lined with a few feathers and bits of animal fur, but more often, the eggs are simply laid on the woody debris at the bottom of the cavity. In British

Columbia, most records of this owl occur between 4 May and 22 October (Howie and Ritcey 1987) and the earlier dates are when pairs are presumed to be on nesting territories. In Washington, nesting activity begins in late April and may run into October (Rodrick and Milner 1991).

Eggs and Young. The eggs are white (Godfrey 1986) and approximately 1.2 x 1.0 inches (30.5 x 25.4 mm) (Herron et al. 1985). The female apparently performs all incubation duties while the male attends the nest from time to time to bring food to the female. Egg dates for 6 clutches ranged from 31 May to 23 July and clutch size ranged from 1 to 4 eggs, with 4 having 2 eggs, and brood size (n=9) ranged from 1 to 4 young (Campbell et al. 1990).

Hunting Behavior and Diet. This small owl opportunistically preys mostly on insects such as moths and grasshoppers along with other arthropods such as spiders, scorpions, and centipedes, which are gleaned from the bark or from the ground. Flying insects may be captured in flight or followed until they alight, then captured (McCallum 1994b). Preferred food in the dry, open forests of eastern Washington were moths and beetles, which are common to abundant (Smith et al. 1997). In Oregon, food of Flammulated Owls consisted mostly of moths and grasshoppers, which were captured along the edges of clearings, in open woodland stands, or in adjacent grasslands and meadows (Goggans 1985; Marshall 1992a).

Territory and Density. The tiny Flammulated Owl maintains a very small home range during the breeding season, and may even form loose colonies. Home ranges of pairs measured during the breeding season averaged about 25 acres (10 ha) on the Starkey Experimental Forest in northeastern Oregon (Goggans 1985). Surveys of Flammulated Owls near Kamloops, British Columbia, revealed

densities of singing males averaging 0.3-0.5 owls per 100 acres (40 ha). These surveys further revealed varying densities between years and an aggregated pattern of distribution (Howie and Ritcey 1980). Several researchers have noted that Flammulated Owls may form loose breeding colonies but whether these are a response to limited habitat availability or a genuine social structure is not known.

Surveys. This is one of the most nocturnal of all owls, being rarely, if ever spotted in daylight hours or even at dusk. It responds fairly readily to calls and is most efficiently surveyed by broadcasts of tape-recorded calls which will provide some information on territory selection and also on local densities. However, it also responds readily to vocal imitations and Flammulateds can be heard singing up to 1 km (0.6 mi) away on quiet evenings (Reynolds and Linkhart 1984). In northeastern Oregon, Bull et al. (1990) established 26 routes spaced 0.2-0.3 mile (0.3-0.5 km) apart totaling 138 miles (220 km) for each of two years. Stops were made every 0.2 miles (0.3 km) for 5 minute periods to listen for vocalizations, and vocal imitations were given if none were heard. During the day, researchers returned to areas within 0.3 mile (0.5 km) of where individuals were heard at night and scratched the bark of trees with potential nest holes so that the owls would reveal themselves. If an owl was detected in a cavity in June and July it was considered nesting. To locate nests, Reynolds and Linkhart (1984) marked all trees containing potential cavities (>1.6 inches or 4 cm) in their study area and used a "cavity peeper" (DeWeese et al. 1975) to assess the suitability of cavities, when possible. Potential cavities were then observed at night for 10 to 15 minutes each to determine occupancy by highlighting cavity entrances against the night sky.

Conservation and Management.
Flammulated Owl distribution in the Pacific Northwest is limited to mature and old-growth

Flammulated Owl.

conifer and mixed forests dominated by ponderosa pine and Douglas fir. This habitat requirement limits their range and distribution. Their distribution and status is unknown over much of its suspected range but this may reflect inadequate sampling, especially along the more remote and rugged areas of montane forest that the Flammulated Owl seems to prefer. Management recommendations for this owl were summarized by Rodrick and Milner (1991) and include the need to: (1) maintain and protect dense old-growth or mature stands near brushy clearings, (2) maintain a minimum of 8 or more snags at least 12 inches (30 cm) in diameter and 6 feet (1.8 m) tall per 100 acres (40 ha) to provide a suitable density of nesting cavities, (3) prevent harvesting or other destruction of trees with cavities and snags needed for nesting cavities, and (4) avoid application of insecticides within the home ranges. Additional conservation measures proposed to protect this species in Oregon include the need to preserve grasslands adjacent to breeding and roosting locations for food, retention of suitable snags for nesting, and buffers against timber harvesting around known or suspected breeding locales (Goggans 1985; Marshall 1992a).

WESTERN SCREECH-OWL *(Otus kennicotti)*
Length 8"; Wingspan 22"

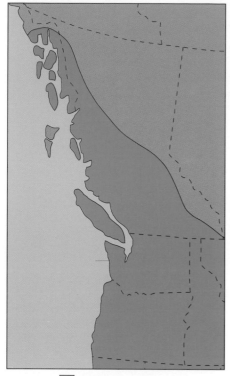

Resident Range

Range. The Western Screech-Owl occurs throughout Oregon, Washington, and southern British Columbia at low to moderate elevations. In British Columbia its range and breeding activity is limited to primarily coastal and southern locales, and rarely at higher elevations. Campbell et al. (1990) for example, reported that no nests were found above 1,770 feet (540 m). The species also occurs locally along the southern coast of Vancouver Island, but is absent from Queen Charlotte Islands. In Oregon and Washington, it is limited primarily to forested regions of low elevation, but east of the Cascades they are mostly confined to towns and riparian areas (Smith et al. 1997; Csuti et al. 1997). Throughout most of its range in the Pacific Northwest, the Western Screech-Owl is a permanent, year-round resident.

Status. All survey information suggests that the status of the Western Screech-Owl in the Pacific Northwest has remained essentially unchanged. It is considered common throughout the western states and is not listed as threatened or endangered by any state (Marks and Marti 1989). However, in British Columbia, the *macfarlanei* subspecies is Red-Listed and the *saturatus* subspecies is Blue-Listed.

Habitat Requirements. The Western Screech-Owl is an owl of open and semi-open habitats such as farmlands, open woodlands (deciduous and mixed forest), and riparian habitats along streams and around lakes and wetlands. This small, nocturnal owl is more tolerant of human activity and human modified landscapes and may take up residence in city gardens, parks and other open space habitats of suburban areas (Smith et al. 1997). Conversely, the Western Screech-Owl becomes rarer in dense coniferous woodlands and at higher elevations, especially northward. In most of Washington, except the central Columbia Basin, Smith et al. (1997) noted that the Western Screech-Owl was a fairly common breeding species in the mixed woodlands and hardwoods, riparian, and even tree-lined city streets and other urban open space.

Nesting. Nest sites are typically located in tree cavities, but vine tangles, buildings, and crevices in cliffs may also be used if natural cavities are not readily available. Natural nest sites in British Columbia were located in either natural cavities or in holes excavated by Pileated Woodpeckers and Northern Flickers and were in black cottonwood, red alder, Douglas fir, western red cedar, and western hemlock (Campbell et al. 1990). However, the majority of nestings (87%) that were

Western Screech-Owl.

reported were in nest boxes. Height of nest cavities varies widely, ranging from 4.2 to 40 feet (1.2 to 12.2 m) in British Columbia but the great majority (65%) are located between 11 to 15 feet (3.4 to 4.6 m) in height (Campbell et al. 1990). While the nest substrate usually consists of wood chips, most nests are generally neither excavated further nor decorated, although they include a slight nest hollow or scrape that contains feathers, animal fur and perhaps mosses which may be brought to line the nest.

Eggs and Young. The eggs are white (Godfrey 1986) and average about 1.4 x 1.2 inches (35.6 x 30.5 mm) in size (Herron et al. 1985). Egg dates for 49 clutches in British Columbia ranged from 17 March to 31 May, clutch size for 51 clutches ranged from 1 to 5 eggs with 73% having 2 or 3 eggs, and brood size for 46 broods ranged from 1 to 5 young with 63% of broods having 2 or 3 young (Campbell et al. 1990).

Roosting. Roost sites during the nonbreeding season seem to be dependent only upon what is immediately available and offers cover at the end of the night. Nest boxes, tree cavities, grape tangles, crevices in cliffs, old buildings, and other structures may be used but this small owl will also roost quietly in trees, if the foliage provides a sufficiently dense cover during the daylight hours.

Hunting Behavior and Diet. The Western Screech-Owl is an opportunistic nocturnal aerial predator that takes a variety of food, depending on local and seasonal availability. Mice, small birds, and larger insects are the most common prey items, but earthworms, crayfish and other invertebrates may also be taken (Bent 1938). In the Puget Sound area, these tiny owls may continue to feed on arthropods well into winter, including: cutworms, crickets, beetles, and centipedes (Bent 1938). Winter food habits in Utah revealed about 50% birds, 25% mammals, and 25% insects (Smith and Wilson

1971). When food is abundant, Screech-Owls may cache extra food in unused tree cavities or sometimes in the nest or roosting site itself. Prey is most often obtained by hunting from low perches and making short dives or stoops to catch rodents or birds but this owl may also glean insects from branches and leaves.

Territory and Density. Little is known about the territory and home range of this owl in the Pacific Northwest. In Arizona, pairs were often spaced as close as 130 to 165 feet (45 to 50 m) apart in riparian habitat, but the surrounding uplands rarely supported a pair for every 900 feet (275 m) (Johnson et al. 1979). Pairs may occupy the same territory throughout the year, but territorial defense is generally absent or greatly lessened from late summer into winter.

Survey Methods. Population surveys can be conducted by using nocturnal broadcasts of tape-recorded calls (Smith et al. 1987).

Determinations of nesting status and productivity of nests is, however, considerably more difficult because of its habit of using concealed sites, typically in tree cavities and therefore information on breeding productivity is sparse.

Conservation and Management. The unchanging status of the Western Screech-Owl lies in its opportunism in prey selection and habitat selection. They are tolerant of human modified landscapes and can successfully roost, nest, and forage in an exceptionally wide variety of habitats. Habitat management priorities for this species include the retention of snags and old trees with cavities suitable for nesting and roosting. The most significant threat to habitat is destruction of riparian zones, but in some cases this impact can be mitigated by providing nest boxes (Marti and Marks 1989). Call (1979) illustrates several types of nest boxes that will work if placed in woodlots or clumps of trees.

Western Screech-Owl from Oregon.

GREAT HORNED OWL *(Bubo virginianus)*
Length 20"; Wingspan 55"

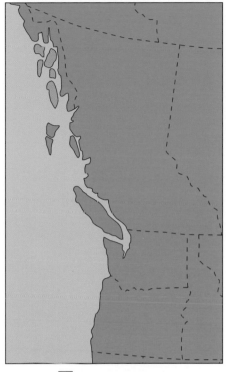

Resident Range

Adult Great Horned Owl
from the Portland area.

Range. This large owl is common and widespread throughout much of Washington and Oregon, excepting only the high-elevation alpine areas of the mountains, the more heavily urbanized areas, barren ground areas, and estuarine mudflats. The distribution of this species in British Columbia is more sporadic, as numbers decrease somewhat northward and in the interior (Campbell et al. 1990). Although the Great Horned Owl is common and widespread in almost all habitats of the Pacific Northwest, breeding abundance is most pronounced in central and northern Oregon, southeastern Washington and central British Columbia (Price et al. 1995). They occur from sea level to elevations of 5,000 feet (1,525 m) on the slopes of Mount Rainier and to about 5,500 feet (1,675 m) at Rogers Lake in the Okanogan Highlands (Smith et al. 1997).

Status. Little is known about the abundance and population trends of the Great Horned Owl in the Pacific Northwest, but there are no known significant threats to their populations in the region (Forsman and Bull 1989). Numbers of this species appear sufficiently common and stable throughout favorable habitats of Washington, Oregon, and British Columbia, and it is not listed in these areas.

Habitat Requirements. The Great Horned Owl is a generalist in habitat requirements throughout its range and can be found nesting from desert shrub to treeline edge of tundra and alpine areas, to urban and suburban open space habitats in the middle of cities and suburbs (Houston et al. 1998). It is most abundant in the gallery forests along rivers and streams, in lightly-wooded hills, in open and semi-open areas of the Palouse Prairie, and farmlands throughout the entire Pacific Northwest. It is much less abundant in the interior of old-growth forests such as the temperate rain forests along the coast. This owl is an edge species that does extremely well in the mosaic of habitats that occur in farmland landscapes, and it even nests, hunts, and roosts in extensive areas of farmland, provided sufficient trees or other suitable nesting substrates are available. In British Columbia, it breeds in an equally wide variety of habitats, in dense or open woodlands, particularly those bordering lakes and marshes and other edge habitats (Campbell et al. 1990).

Nesting. This large, aggressive owl nests in old nests of hawks, especially Red-tailed, Ferruginous, Swainson's, and Cooper's Hawks, and occasionally in the nests of Northern Goshawk, Raven, Common Crow, magpie, or squirrel. It may occasionally usurp a nest from a Red-tailed Hawk pair during or shortly after they have completed most of its construction. If nests of other species are unavailable, these owls have been known to nest in cliff niches, rocky outcrops, badlands, shallow caves, bridge and pier abutments, and snags, and in the tops of broken trees (Houston et al. 1998). Cavities in rocky outcrops and along cliff lines are readily used when available. More rarely they will choose a nest in an oversized tree cavity, or in an abandoned building. Knight and Smith (1982) noted 6 cliff nests and one tree nest along the Esquatzel Coulee in southeastern Washington and Knight et al. (1982) noted 5 cliff nests and 8 tree nests along the Columbia River in north-central Washington. Campbell et al. (1990) noted that Great Horned Owls in British Columbia chose crevices in cliffs, clay banks, and structures. Tree nests predominated, and of 75 tree nests, 57% were in conifers and the remainder in deciduous trees, mostly black cottonwood (21%) and quaking aspen (9%) while nest heights of 67 tree nests ranged from 5 to 112 feet (1.5 to 34 m) above ground (Campbell et al. 1990). If suitable elevated nest sites are unavailable, these owls may even use ground nests, as found at Malheur National Wildlife Refuge in southeastern Oregon (Littlefield 1990) albeit extremely rarely. Nests are generally unadorned, although the female may line them with downy feathers. Cliff and ground nests consist of a simple scrape sparsely lined with a few feathers.

Eggs and Young. The eggs are white (Godfrey 1986) and average about 2.2 x 1.8 inches (55.9 x 45.7 mm) in size (Herron et al. 1985). Great Horned Owl nesting begins early throughout the Pacific Northwest with clutches generally being laid in late February or early March. Egg dates for 38 clutches in British Columbia ranged from 15 February to 20 May with 50% being found between 24 February and 18 March (Campbell et al. 1990). Clutch size for 35 clutches ranged from 1 to 4 eggs, with 71% having two eggs and brood size for 203 broods ranged from 1 to 4 young with 54% having 2 young (Campbell et al. 1990). Young are generally recorded from late March into late May or June.

Roost Sites and Roosting. As with nesting sites, Great Horned Owls have been recorded using an exceptionally wide variety of roosting sites. Favorite roosting sites are in trees, especially conifers and other species that provide good cover, but this owl may also roost in swamps, shrub-covered wetlands, old buildings, or among the girders and support structures of bridges and railroad trestles (Houston et al. 1998).

Hunting Behavior and Diet. Great Horned Owls are exceptionally opportunistic predators and will take an extremely wide variety of prey (Houston et al. 1998).
Small to medium-sized mammals are

typically their staple prey, especially rabbits, ground squirrels, tree squirrels, rats, voles, and mice, but almost any mammal up to and including the size of small foxes, porcupines, racoons, marmots, and house cats have been recorded as prey of this large and powerful owl. A wide variety of birds are taken as prey, including: (1) waterbirds incubating on nests or roosting on water, (2) landbirds that roost in the open at night, (3) birds that forage at night (including owls), (4) nestlings stolen from nests, and (5) adult birds incubating on nests (including most hawks). Other prey may include amphibians, fish, insects and other invertebrates. Overall, the average prey weight calculated for Great Horned Owls in eastern Washington was 55 grams (Knight and Jackman 1984). These powerful owls hunt primarily by perch hunting, making short flights (< 100 yards or meters) only after prey has been detected (Johnsgard 1988). They are mainly crepuscular and nocturnal in their hunting, but may hunt occasionally during the day in the breeding season (TB, DGS).

Portrait of a Great Horned Owl found near Portland, Oregon.

Territory and Density. Great Horned Owls are highly territorial during the breeding season and home ranges are fairly large, about a square mile in area. In the Yukon territory, average home range size for 10 territorial adults was 615 acres (248 ha) (Rohner 1997). In north-central Washington, Knight et al. (1982) noted an average distance between nests of 2.4 miles (3.9 km) along the Columbia River.

Survey Methods. In open country, nesting Great Horned Owls can be surveyed by observing raptor nests prior to leaf-out or by checking cliffs for crevices or raptor nests on ledges. Nests can also be located following the procedures of Craighead and Craighead (1956) by driving available roads or walking through woodlots and examining nest structures for signs of activity (whitewash, feathers, eggshells, prey remains). In large woodlots and heavily-forested areas, surveys can be conducted using broadcasts

of tape-recorded calls (Kochert 1986; Mosher et al. 1990). Territorial individuals and pairs will generally respond to broadcasts, signaling the presence of a home range. Responsiveness is greatest to this method in fall and early spring, when pairs are claiming new territories or reestablishing old territories. Broadcast surveys may be conducted at any time of night, but usually the first few hours just after darkness or just before daylight elicit the highest response rates (DGS).

Conservation and Management. The extremely adaptable, abundant, and dominant Great Horned Owl is currently not in need of any conservation or management (Houston et al. 1998). In fact, these aggressive predators routinely feed on other large and small raptors (adults and young) such as Northern Goshawks, Cooper's Hawks, Red-shouldered Hawks, Red-tailed Hawks, Broad-winged Hawks, Barred Owls, and Spotted Owls to name a few (Bent 1937; Crocker-Bedford 1990; Bosakowski and Smith 1992; Rosenfield and Bielefeldt 1993). Great Horneds are often considered a nuisance and a threat in the management of threatened and endangered raptors, and attempts to encourage their nesting should be questioned or discouraged.

Snowy Owl *(Nyctea scandiaca)*
Length 20"; Wingspan 55"

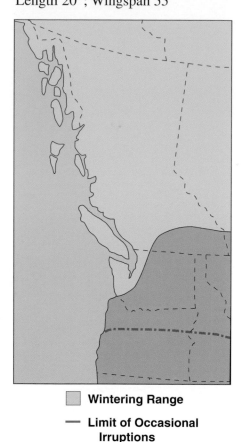

■ **Wintering Range**

— **Limit of Occasional Irruptions**

Range. This circumpolar owl breeds in the northern tundras of the world and winters either within its breeding range or migrates southward, often in spectacular numbers during periodic irruptions. Females and young males more often winter in the southern provinces of Canada and the northern United States. During especially severe winters spectacular irruptions of Snowy Owls may send large numbers of these owls drifting southward (Smith and Ellis 1989). The Snowy Owl is an occasional winter visitor to the Pacific Northwest but their winter abundance decreases south through Washington and into Oregon. In British Columbia, they occur from sea level to at least 6,000 feet (1,830 m) in elevation (Campbell et al. 1990).

Status. The winter status of Snowy Owls in British Columbia varies from fairly common to rare depending on the severity of the influx. In high-movement years, they occur widely along the coast with notable concentrations piling up at southern Vancouver Island and the Fraser River delta, while in the interior they are widely scattered (Campbell et al. 1990). Jewett et al. (1953) categorized the Snowy Owl in Washington as an irregular but cyclic migrant and widespread winter visitor which typically occurred from October 2 to April 13, while in Oregon they are known mostly as cyclical but rare winter visitors to the Willamette Valley region.

Habitat Requirements. These winter visitors are typically found in more open habitats such as fields, grasslands, coastal marshes, coastal dunes, and even the open habitats that surround airports (Parmalee 1992). In Alberta, wintering female Snowy Owls preferred stubble fields and hayfields, and avoided fallow fields (Boxall and Lein 1982a). Campbell et al. (1990) noted that Snowy Owls in interior British Columbia favor grasslands, lakeshores, marshes, and alpine meadows, whereas those that winter along the coast used log-covered beaches, offshore islands, sand dunes, rocky headlands, and human modified habitats such as airports, open parks, landfills, school yards and agricultural landscapes. Perch sites in these winter habitats encompass any elevated spot that provides an overview of the landscape and fence posts, rocks, buildings, towers, and other structures are appropriated, as available (Godfrey 1986; Campbell et al. 1990).

Adult female Snowy Owl.

Hunting Behavior and Diet. The most common hunting technique for wintering Snowy Owls is "still perch" or "sit-and-wait" (Boxall and Lein 1982b). Hunting owls used perches such as utility poles, fence posts, or buildings to scan the area for 10 to 15 minutes and would often move to another perch 300 to 600 feet (100 to 200 m) away if no prey were observed. Occasionally, hovering and low coursing flights are used as hunting methods. Near Calgary, winter diets of adults were comprised mainly of deer mice (45.3%), meadow voles (31.3%), and Richardson's ground squirrels (9.4%) (Boxall and Lein 1982b). Analysis of pellet remains and tabulation of kills in British Columbia have demonstrated this owl's comparatively high use of birds, especially waterbirds (Campbell et al. 1990). Snowy Owl pellets near Victoria, for example, contained entirely birds with a marked concentration on Bufflehead and Horned Grebe (Campbell and MacColl 1978). While another prey analysis conducted by Kennedy et al. (1982) on the Fraser River delta, British Columbia, found that waterfowl and a few other birds comprised 99.8 % biomass of the winter diet. Snowy Owls that winter southward into the northern states feature a much more diverse diet, such as ducks, seabirds, shorebirds, rats, mice, and almost any other small mammals are taken (Smith and Ellis 1989). A hungry Snowy Owl is a formidable bird of prey that can easily capture and kill animals considerably larger than itself. In parts of their winter range, Snowy Owls may take larger mammals and birds such as muskrats, jackrabbits, Ring-necked Pheasant, chickens, geese, wild and domestic turkeys and Great Blue Herons (Parmelee 1992). When food is scarce, Snowy Owls will eat almost anything, including road kills and scraps of garbage (Smith and Ellis 1989).

Territory and Density. Female Snowy Owls may defend large winter territories of

Adult male Snowy Owl.

375 to 1,125 acres (150 to 450 ha) for up to 80 days, whereas males are more nomadic, and occasionally set-up small territories for up to 18 days (Boxall and Lein 1982a).

Survey Methods. In Alberta, long survey routes (40 miles, 64 km) were driven every 2 to 4 weeks by two field workers who drove at a speed of 19-31 mph (30-50 kmph), and stopped every 2.0 miles (3.2 km) to scan the surrounding area with binoculars (Lein and Webber 1979).

Conservation and Management. During their winter movements southward, however, Snowy Owls can have close contact with people and their activities. These owls often congregate at airports where they become a nuisance and sometimes a hazard to aircraft travel (Smith and Ellis 1989). Reduction in illegal shooting and trapping of Snowy Owls either for sport, for trophy hunting, or for depredation losses is also important to their conservation. The local implementation of policies and practices that will also

protect the birds from hazards such as aircraft strikes and electrocutions will also prove beneficial. Changing designs of power poles to prevent electrocution is a management activity that can benefit Snowy Owls and other raptors that like to use these structures as hunting perches (Olendorff et al. 1981).

Snowy Owl.

NORTHERN HAWK OWL *(Surnia ulula)*
Length 14"; Wingspan 33"

Northern Hawk Owl using exposed spruce snag on the south slope of the Brooks range, Alaska.

Resident Range

— **Limit of Occasional Irruptions**

Range. The Northern Hawk Owl breeds in northern British Columbia and southward throughout higher elevations in the Rocky Mountains of British Columbia (Godfrey 1986). It is generally a resident of its breeding range, but may wander south irregularly in winter as far south as the northeastern corner of Washington and casually to western Oregon. Watson et al. (1989) noted two occurrences in Oregon including one at Sauvie Island, near Portland, on 4 November 1973 and one near Palmer Junction, Union County, on 13 January 1983. Breeding has occurred at elevations of 1,800-6,000 feet (550 and 1,830 m) in British Columbia (Campbell et al. 1990).

Status. Very little is known about population size and trends of this diurnal owl that inhabits the remote boreal forest of Canada. Only 16 breeding records exist for northern British Columbia, which includes 3 nests and 13 cases of flightless young (Campbell et al. 1990).

Habitat Requirements. Habitat is characterized as open to moderately-dense boreal forests (coniferous or mixed) that are bordered by marshes, muskegs, or other openings or burnt forestland with standing stubs (Godfrey 1986). In British Columbia, preferred habitats include fairly open coniferous and mixed forests of white spruce, Engelmann spruce, subalpine fir, aspen, birch, and mountain hemlock (Campbell et al. 1990).

Nesting. Nest sites are usually found in hollow tops of dead tree stubs, natural tree cavities and enlarged woodpecker holes, and occasionally old platform nests of crows and hawks are used (Godfrey 1986). Across Canada, Bent (1938) reported nest heights ranging from 5.2 feet (1.6 m) to at least 42.6 feet (13 m). In the Yukon, nest sites were all in spruce snags with 7 located in hollow broken-off tops and 2 located in side cavities where large branches had broken-off leaving a large hole (Rohner et al. 1995). Nest heights ranged from 11.2 to 23.3 feet (3.4 to 7.1 m) above ground. The three known nests from British Columbia were in a hole in a snag, the broken-off top of a tree, and in a cavity near the top of a broken-off spruce tree with nest heights of 15, 20 and 60 feet (4.6, 6.1, and 18.3 m), respectively (Campbell et al. 1990).

Eggs and Young. The eggs are white (Godfrey 1986) and average about 1.6 x 1.3 inches (40.1 x 31.9 mm) in size (Bent 1938). In the Yukon, clutches were initiated between 19 April and 11 May and brood size varied between 2 to 5 with a mean productivity of 3.7 young fledged per nest (Rohner et al. 1995).

Hunting Behavior and Diet. The Northern Hawk Owl is a diurnal hunter, and apparently does not hunt at night. Perch hunting is the most usual method of catching prey whereby the owls launch rapid pursuit flights from elevated perch sites, much like that of *Accipiter* hawks. Hovering is also occasionally used. This owl feeds primarily on small mammals (voles, mice, shrews, lemmings) and insects, but may feed occasionally on ptarmigan (Earhart and Johnson 1970) as well as juvenile

Northern Hawk Owl perched on a telephone wire.

and stressed-adult snowshoe hares (Rohner et al. 1995). In the Yukon, 449 prey items were collected during the breeding season with voles and mice accounting for the bulk of the diet (87.2%), followed by snowshoe hares (6.6%), other small mammals (5.5%), and birds (0.6%) (Rohner et al. 1995).

Territory and Density. This medium-sized owl appears to be territorial and breeds at fairly low densities. Adults will defend their nest by diving at human intruders (Kehoe 1982). A maximum nesting density of 6 nests per 39 square miles (100 square km) was reported for southwestern Yukon, Canada (Rohner et al. 1995). Internest distances as close as 1.12 miles (1.8 km) apart have been reported for North America (Duncan and Duncan 1998).

Survey Methods. Although Hawk Owls are diurnal and conspicuous when perched atop snags or trees, they can be difficult to find in the expansive and largely inaccessible boreal forest. Systematic foot searches have been used to survey Hawk Owls on their breeding grounds in the Yukon (Rohner et al. 1995). When adult birds were located, the observers followed them with prey to locate their nests. In winter, vehicle surveys were conducted along the Alaska Highway for a total of 2,381 hours and an abundance index of Hawk Owls seen per 100 observation hours was calculated (Rohner et al. 1995).

Conservation and Management. More than 50% of breeding habitat for this species is likely non-commercial boreal forest or "forest and barren" areas where northern forests are more open (Duncan and Duncan 1998). In the remaining forests, clear-cutting may increase prey populations (*Microtus* spp.) and accessibility by hunting owls, but has likely reduced nest site and hunting perch availability. These negative effects can be mitigated somewhat by leaving large residual trees in clearcuts and convoluted edges for feeding, loafing, calling, and nesting (Duncan and Duncan 1998).

NORTHERN PYGMY-OWL *(Glaucidium gnoma)*
Length 6"; Wingspan 15"

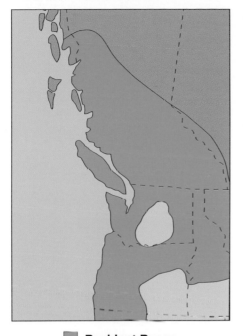

■ **Resident Range**

☐ **WIntering Range**

Range. This tiny owl ranges across western North America from British Columbia southward through Washington and Oregon and southward along the cordillerla into Central America. In Oregon it apparently occurs along the Coast Range, Klamath Mountains, Blue Mountains, Cascade Range, and the ranges in the south-central portion of the state (Marshall 1992a). In British Columbia, it breeds mainly in the southern half of the province and Vancouver Island, but is absent from the Queen Charlotte Islands (Campbell et al. 1990). It is considered a primary resident in this range but individuals may exhibit elevational shifts during fall and winter. Nesting has been reported from from 1,600 to 4,000 feet (490 to 1,220 m) in elevation (Campbell et al. 1990).

Status. The overall status of this small secretive owl is hard to assess because it remains the least known North American

Northern Pygmy-Owl from Oregon.

owl (Reynolds et al. 1989). It is listed as a sensitive species in Oregon because so little is known of its distribution, abundance, and habitat requirements (Marshall 1992a). The Vancouver Island subspecies *swarthi* is currently Blue-Listed in British Columbia.

Habitat Requirements. Northern Pygmy-Owls occur in a wide variety of forest types, from open woodlands to old-growth forests, but they are most commonly observed along forest-edge habitats (Marshall 1992a; Campbell et al. 1990). They also occur in mixed woodlands, orchards, streamside thickets, and less frequently in urban open space and residential areas (Campbell et al. 1990). On an industrial forest in the western Washington Cascades, Northern Pygmy Owls showed a positive regression for only one type of habitat, alder-hardwood forest, albeit the sample size was very small (n=4) (Bosakowski 1997). On the Olympic Peninsula, 9 radiotagged individuals showed use of all cover types, but mature structurally complex habitats were used more than younger structurally simple habitats (Giese 1999). Furthermore, these radiotagged owls did not preferentially occur along edges, although there was some evidence that nest sites tended to be positioned near edges.

Nesting. The Pygmy-Owl nests in natural and excavated tree cavities in both conifers and hardwoods. In Oregon, nests were reported in cavities excavated by flickers, sapsuckers, and acorn woodpecker (Marshall 1992a). Similarly, five nests found in British Columbia were all located in woodpecker holes (Campbell et al. 1990). Bull et al. (1987) found two nest sites in Oregon, one in a dead Douglas-fir stand near a meadow while the second nest was in a grand fir about 1,700 yards from a partial cut. Reynolds et al. (1989) noted that nests had been found in mature and old-growth Douglas fir and western red cedar along Oregon's coast range while Bent (1938) noted that early naturalists had also found

them in aspen cavities. Nest height for 18 nests averaged 20.6 feet (6.3 m) above ground, ranging from 7.5 to 65.6 feet (2.3-20 m) (Johnsgard 1988). Most known nests have been found in deciduous trees, with 6 in sycamores, 4 in pines, 3 in oaks, 2 in firs, and one each in locust, cedar, alder, and cottonwood (Johnsgard 1988). Nests contained a base of wood chips and one was lined with western red cedar bark (Campbell et al. 1990).

Eggs and Young. The eggs are white (Godfrey 1986) and average about 1.2 x 0.96 inches (29.6 x 24.3 mm) in size (Bent 1938). Clutch size for 18 clutches ranged from 3 to 5 eggs, with an average of 3.2 eggs (Johnsgard 1988). Pygmy-Owls are among the few owl species that do not begin incubation until the entire clutch is complete. Brood size for 11 broods ranged from 1 to 7 young (Campbell et al. 1990) with an average of 3.1 young.

Hunting Behavior and Diet. The Pygmy-Owl diet is comprised mainly of insects and small vertebrates. The long list of vertebrates includes representatives of small mammals, birds, reptiles, and amphibians. Pygmy-Owl prey recorded in Oregon by Bull et al. (1987) included shrews (*Sorex* spp.), voles (*Microtus* spp. and *Phenacomys intermedius*), deer mice, and sparrows along with a mix of insects. Although Pygmy-Owls normally prey on small vertebrates they have been recorded attacking larger birds such as California Quail (Balgooyen 1969). This tiny owl is essentially a diurnal and crepuscular hunter and uses surprise attacks, as it glides down swiftly from some elevated perch (Johnsgard 1988).

Territory and Density. There is no specific published information on the territories and breeding densities of these tiny owls in the Pacific Northwest. Northern Pygmy-Owls were located during breeding bird surveys at 4 of 330 point count stations, which sampled approximately 25,594 acres (10,362 ha) of a 54,000-acre (21,600-ha) private industrial forest in the western Washington Cascades (Bosakowski 1997).

Survey Methods. Northern Pygmy-Owls can be located during breeding bird surveys using standard point count methods. In one study, 4 of 330 point count stations were occupied (1.2% occupancy) on an industrial forest in the western Washington Cascades (Bosakowski 1997). Singing occurred from dawn to mid-morning (TB), such that point counts for breeding birds may represent a useful tool for establishing population indices for this little known owl species. Use of broadcasted conspecific calls is a technique (Kochert 1986) that also could be applied to surveying Pygmy-Owls since it may help augment detection rates.

Conservation and Management. Partial forest clearing may improve hunting opportunities (Johnsgard 1988), but its dependence on woodpecker holes and other natural cavities may be a limiting factor if too many large diameter, diseased or decaying trees are removed during timber harvest or firewood collections (Reynolds et al. 1989). In addition, aerial spraying of carbaryl insectides to reduce forest pests might affect abundance of non-target insects that serve as prey for Pygmy-Owls (Reynolds et al. 1989).

Streamside habitat with mixed woodlands of conifers and hardwoods.

BURROWING OWL *(Athene cunicularia)*
Length 8"; Wingspan 22"

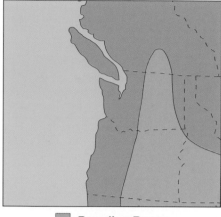

Breeding Range

Burrowing Owl at nest burrow.

GERRIT VYN

Range. The Burrowing Owl ranges from southern British Columbia southward through the prairie grasslands and sagebrush steppe of Washington and Oregon. In British Columbia, breeding is limited to the central-southern interior from Kamloops south to the Okanagan and Similkameen Valleys, locally along the coast at the Fraser River delta (Campbell et al. 1990) and nests have been found from 6.6 feet (2 m) below sea level to 1,395 feet (425 m) inland. Burrowing Owls that nest in northern areas migrate southward into the southwestern United States and some reach as far south as Guatemala and El Salvador. However, a few have been detected on Christmas Bird Counts in the Columbia Basin of Washington (Smith and Knight 1981).

Status. Formerly a widespread species in suitable open habitats of the western range, Burrowing Owls have been declining throughout much of their range in the Pacific Northwest. They were Blue-Listed from 1971-1982 and again in 1986. In the Pacific Northwest they are Red-Listed in British Columbia and considered to be seriously declining within their range in eastern Washington (Smith et al. 1997). Numbers in

Oregon have also been steadily declining. It is considered a federal species of concern, a state candidate species in Washington, a species of concern in Oregon, and is Red-Listed in British Columbia. Population declines have been linked to loss of habitat, especially former prairie dog and ground squirrel colonies which have periodically been eradicated via local poisoning campaigns. Smith et al. (1997) reported that the primary factors limiting this species in Washington were lack of suitable nest sites, especially the loss of Columbia ground squirrel colonies which were a major source of burrows. To illustrate, the conversion of natural open landscapes to agricultural farmlands in southern Walla Walla County, Washington, was implicated in the loss of eight Burrowing Owl breeding sites.

Habitat Requirements. The primary landscape features consistent with Burrowing Owl breeding areas are drier, treeless habitats in shrub-steppe, short-grass prairies, and semi-arid sagebrush desert scrub (Campbell et al. 1990; Smith et al. 1997). Burrowing Owls are tolerant of and respond well to human-modi-fied landscapes and even human landscapes and can be found occupying such open habi-tats as airport lawns, college campuses, ceme-teries, maintained powerline rights of way, and golf courses (Haug et al. 1993). On the British Columbia coast, short-grass, reclaimed agricultural land is inhabited (Campbell et al. 1990).

Nesting. Burrowing Owls nest in small to large colonies where sufficient habitat and food is available, but isolated pairs are com-monly seen where suitable open habitat is patchy. Both sexes participate in selecting a nesting site, which is usually an old badger or fox burrow, with a mound that provides an elevated perch site for territory advertisement. Pairs do not excavate their own nest burrows, but may enlarge old burrows and also the nest cavity within the burrow. Nest sites in eastern Washington included rocky outcroppings,

ground squirrel burrows, and drain pipes (Smith et al. 1997). In British Columbia, bur-rows from yellow-bellied marmot, badger, striped skunk, and Belted Kingfisher were used as well as an old drain pipe and a crevice in a railroad embankment (Campbell et al. 1990). Artificial burrows constructed by local wildlife organizations have also been used (Smith et al. 1997). The female often lines the nest with feathers, cow chips and other dried manure, bits of mud, pellet remains, occasion-ally grasses and animal fur.

Eggs and Young. The eggs are white, often nest-stained (Godfrey 1986) and average about 1.2 x 1.0 inches (30.5 x 25.4 mm) in size (Herron et al. 1985). Egg dates for 5 clutches in British Columbia ranged from 6 May to 24 May, and clutch size ranged from 6 to 10 eggs, and brood size for 12 broods ranged from 1 to 6 young, with 7 broods hav-ing 4 or 5 young (Campbell et al. 1990).

Hunting Behavior and Diet. Burrowing Owls are primarily crepuscular in their hunt-ing, but will feed at any hour of the day or

Burrowing Owl.

night. These ground-dwellers hunt by walking, hopping, or running or by perch hunting, fly-catching, and hovering a few feet above ground (Haug et al. 1993). They feed mostly on insects and other invertebrates, and occasionally small mammals, mostly rodents, lizards, snakes, turtles, toads, frogs, crustaceans and small birds. In Oregon, invertebrates represented 91.6% of the diet by frequency, but only 22% by biomass, whereas small vertebrates (mostly mammals) represented 8.4% by frequency, but 78% by biomass (Green 1983).

Territory and Density. The Burrowing Owl is a semi-colonial species, often forming loose colonies and breeding at high densities (Haug et al. 1993). Feeding areas are not defended, but pairs defend their own nest burrows. Pairs may advertise their territory by perching on the selected mound or nearby fence posts or telephone poles or other elevated sites. Home range size for 6 radiotagged males varied from 35 to 1188 acres (14 to 481 ha) in Saskatchewan, but diurnal activities were restricted to within 820 feet (250 m) of the nest burrow (Haug et al. 1993).

Survey Methods. Burrowing Owls are surveyed by driving available roads or hiking, and searching for any type of rodent colony (prairie dogs, ground squirrel) and scanning areas in early morning and late afternoon for owls that might be perching atop mounds, brush, fence posts, or telephone lines (Call 1978).

Conservation and Management. Protection of existing nesting colonies is a key conservation measure and conversion of adjacent areas to suitable habitat can provide new habitat patches for these existing colonies (Trulio 1997). Burrowing Owls will also use artificial nests in suitable open country habitats. For example, several artificial burrows constructed in the Potholes area of east-central Washington were successfully utilized by the owls as nest sites (Smith et al. 1997). These artificial burrows work well if placed near other active burrows (passive relocation), but large-scale reintroduction programs to formerly occupied historic sites have failed to date (Trulio 1997). Call (1979) illustrates the design of an artificial burrow made with PVC pipe and an underground nest box.

Burrowing Owl nest and view of habitat near Yakima Firing Range, Washington.

SPOTTED OWL *(Strix occidentalis)*
Length 16"; Wingspan 42"

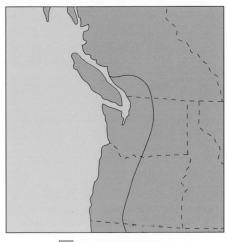

Resident Range

Spotted Owl in old-growth Douglas firs from Gifford-Pinchot National Forest just south of Mt. Rainier near Packwood.

Range. The Northern Spotted Owl (*caurina* subspecies) ranges along Pacific coast forests throughout the Cascade and Coast Ranges of Oregon and Washington, the Olympic Peninsula, (Forsman and Bull 1989) and extreme southwestern British Columbia, north to Alta Lake, east to Hope and Manning Provincial Park (Godfrey 1986). Elevations ranged from 80 feet (24 m) above sea level to 4,400 feet (1,341 m) in the northern Cascades and 6,600 feet (2,012 m) in the southern Cascades (Forsman et al. 1984).

Status. The subspecies *caurina* is rare in British Columbia and declining in Oregon and Washington. It is classified as federally-threatened in the United States (USDI 1990), endangered in Washington, threatened in Oregon, and Red-Listed in British Columbia. Models predict that loss of mature and old-growth forests due to commercial logging and subsequent forest fragmentation are key factors in the decline of this forest owl (Doak 1989; Thomas et al. 1990).

Habitat Requirements. In the Pacific Northwest, the Northern Spotted Owl inhabits primarily old-growth coniferous forest (Forsman et al. 1984, 1987; Thomas et al. 1990; Carey et al. 1990; Hershey et al. 1998). Suitable habitat for spotted owls is generally considered to be mature or old-growth forest, exhibiting the following characteristics: moderate to high canopy closure; a multi-layered, multi-species canopy dominated by large overstory trees, a high incidence of large trees with various deformities such as cavities, broken tops, and dwarf mistletoe infections; large accumulations of fallen trees and woody debris on the ground; numerous large snags; and sufficient open space below the canopy for owls to fly (Thomas et al. 1990). This definition of nesting-foraging-roosting (NRF) habitat generally describes classic old-growth forest (Franklin et al. 1981) of which continues to shrink in acreage each year. On a landscape basis, owl nest sites in Oregon contained significantly more old-conifer forest than random sites at all four plot sizes that were tested including 295, 1178, 2642, and 4565 acres (118, 471, 1057, and 1826 ha) (Ripple et al. 1997). Further studies by Swindle et al. (1999) reported that nests were associated with higher proportions of old forest near the nest. Bart and Forsman (1992) found that spotted owls are rare and have low productivity in younger forests (50-80 years old). However, Spotted Owls will use younger forest seral stages for roosting, foraging, and dispersal (Thomas et al. 1990). During transient dispersal, juvenile use of old forest (35%) was similar to availability (31%), but during the settling phase of dispersal, called colonization, use of old forest (61%) was nearly double compared

to availability (33%) (Miller et al. 1997). These results suggest that older forests were only specifically selected at the end of the juvenile dispersal process when young were settling into potential future nesting areas. High canopy closure (>80%) was a consistent feature of nest sites and foraging sites in younger, managed forests (Irwin et al. 2000).

Nesting. In Westside forests, Spotted Owls nest primarily in large old trees and snags with large hollow cavities or broken-off tops. Of 47 nests studied in Oregon, 64% were in cavities and broken tops and the remaining nests were in stick platforms or on other debris (Forsman et al. 1984). Similar trends were found on the Olympic Peninsula, where 105 of 116 nests were in cavities and only 11 were on external platforms on tree limbs (Forsman and Geise 1997). However, in eastside forests, stick platforms (old goshawk nests) were most commonly used for nesting (55.3%), along with mistletoe platforms (24.7%), cavities (10.6%), broken-tops (5.9%), and large branches (3.5%) (Buchanan et al. 1993).

Eggs and Young. The eggs are white (Godfrey 1986) and average about 2.0 x 1.6 inches (49.9 x 41.3 mm) in size (Bent 1938). In Oregon, clutch size was 2 eggs in 4 clutches examined and an average of 1.4 young were produced per successful nesting attempt (Forsman et al. 1984). Most owlets leave the nest as branchers when they are 32 to 36 days old and can make short flights when they are 40 to 45 days old (Forsman et al. 1984).

Hunting Behavior and Diet. Spotted Owls hunt primarily by using a perch hunting technique where they dive upon prey from low-elevated perches and may hop along the ground after a fleeing prey animal (Forsman et al. 1984). In Oregon, more than 4,500 prey items were examined including 31 mammal species, 23 bird species, 2 reptile species and several invertebrates

Spotted Owl from Gifford-Pinchot National Forest in Washington.

GERRIT VYN

Spotted Owl habitat: old-growth coniferous forest at Mount Rainier National Park, Washington.

(Forsman et al. 1984). Overall, the northern flying squirrel was the most important prey item by frequency and biomass. Flying squirrels were also the most preferred prey item in the eastern Cascade Range of Washington near Cle Elum (Bevis et al. 1997). In a recent Washington study, northern flying squirrels were the most important prey species in most areas of the Olympic Peninsula, western Cascades, and eastern Cascades (Forsman et al. 2001). In addition, snowshoe hares (mostly juvenile), bushytailed woodrats, boreal red-backed voles and mice (*Peromyscus* spp.) were other important prey species.

Territory and Density. Spotted Owls are territorial and have enormous home ranges which have a tendency to increase in size in more northern latitudes or at higher elevations. In northern Washington, 10 radiotagged Spotted Owls had a mean summer home range size of 4,014 acres (1,625 ha) (Hamer et al. 1989). In the southern Oregon coast range, a mean home range size ranging

from 2,848 to 9,744 acres (1,121 to 3,944 ha) was revealed for four pairs of Spotted Owls (Carey et al. 1990).

Survey Methods. The Spotted Owl can be readily surveyed by broadcasting taped calls or by using vocal imitations of their simple four-note call (who, hoo-hoo, whoaw). Call (1978) recommended conducting systematic searches of suitable old-growth forest, and broadcasting taped calls every quarter-mile. Calling inventories by Hamer et al. (1989) were conducted by driving along forest roads and stopping every 1/3 mile (540 meters) to call and listen for owls. Where hiking trails and unroaded areas were surveyed on foot, calls were given every few minutes as previously described by Forsman et al. (1977). Standard call-survey protocols have been designed for the management of this threatened species in areas subject to timber harvesting (USDA 1988a).

Conservation and Management. With less than 10% of the original old-growth forest remaining in the Pacific Northwest (Bolsinger and Waddell 1993), a recovery plan was instituted for the Northern Spotted Owl population (U.S. Fish and Wildlife Service 1992). From that report, a series of options for ecosystem management were developed (FEMAT 1993). Finally, one of those options for managing late-succession-al and old-growth forests in the range of the owl was adopted (USDA and USDI 1994) and is referred to as The President's Forest Plan or Northwest Forest Plan. This com-plex plan is based on the premise that most of the remaining habitat is on federal land and that strict conservation and manage-ment of these forests will protect the remaining Spotted Owl population. However, recent attempts to skirt around the plan, such as the Salvage Logging Rider, could damage the effectiveness of the plan in maintaining population viability for the owl. Habitat management for Spotted Owls is accomplished by delineation of habitat

within "owl circles", which represent the mean home range sizes of about 3,650 hectares (9,016 acres) in Washington and 1,810 hectares (4,471 acres) in Oregon (USDA 1988b). Owls are located by stan-dard call-survey protocols, and around nests (or activity centers), at least 40% suitable habitat (nesting, roosting, foraging) must be maintained within a 2.1-mile (3.4 km) radius for Washington and a 1.5-mile (2.4 km) radius for Oregon (USDA 1988b). However, the adequacy of the circle method is suspect (Lehmkuhl and Raphael 1993) because owls may adjust the shape of their ranges to include as much old-growth as possible (Carey et al. 1992). In addition to habitat loss, hybridization with Barred Owls to form "Sparred Owl" hybrids has occurred (Hamer et al. 1989; Hamer et al. 1994; Smith et al. 1997) which could threaten the genetic integrity of future spotted owl popu-lations, and Barred Owls are likely to increase competition for food.

Spotted Owl from Gifford-Pinchot National Forest in Washington.

BARRED OWL *(Strix varia)*
Length 17"; Wingspan 44"

Resident Range

Range. The Barred Owl ranges throughout most of British Columbia (mostly southern and eastern), all forested regions of Washington, the Cascade, Coast and Blue mountains of Oregon, and the northwestern tip of California (Hamer et al. 1989; Csuti et al. 1997). It has been recorded at elevations up to 4,000 (1,220 m) in Columbia County, Washington (Smith et al. 1997). Breeding evidence has been documented at elevations of between 300 to 3,600 (90 to 1,100 m) in British Columbia (Campbell et al. 1990).

Status. Over the past 30 years, the Barred Owl has colonized most forested regions in the Pacific Northwest. Although specific population numbers are not available, this owl is steadily increasing (Forsman and Bull 1989) and expanding its range.

Habitat Requirements. The Barred Owl is a forest owl which occurs in mixed or coniferous forests, usually near water, including

Barred Owl.

swamps, streams, lakeshores, creek valleys, or river bottoms (Campbell et al. 1990). In the central Cascade Range, Barred Owl densities were greater on the wetter, west-side forests, but in drier eastside forests, these owls were found associated with river and stream corridors, forested wetlands, and higher elevations receiving higher rainfall (Herter and Hicks 2000). In Alberta, these owls were largely restricted to the mixed-wood boreal forest and further south in montane and foothill forest with few in the aspen parkland and none in the scattered wooded areas of prairie (Boxall and Stepney 1982). In central Saskatchewan, Barred Owl home ranges had greater proportions of older mixed-wood forest (80+ years) than available habitats (Mazur et al. 1998). Radiotelemetry studies in Washington have discovered that Barred Owls use less old-growth habitat than Spotted Owls and use more pole and small sawtimber forests, but overlap in old-

Barred Owl.

growth forest does occur (Hamer et al. 1989).

Nesting. Nests have been found in live trees in natural tree cavities and in snags with broken-off tops. Of 11 nests examined in Washington, all were located in tree cavities of western red cedar (Hamer et al. 1989). In western Washington, a nest was reported in a dense 80-year-old stand of mixed hardwood/conifer forest in a cavity of a big-leaf maple (Leder and Walters 1980). In British Columbia, 8 nests have been found including 4 in the broken-off tops of Douglas-fir, and 4 in natural cavities in black cottonwoods, and nest heights for all nests ranged from 20 to 98 feet (6 to 30 m) (Campbell et al. 1990).

Eggs and Young. The eggs are plain white (Godfrey 1986) and average about 1.9 x 1.7 inches (49 x 42 mm) in size (Bent 1938). Clutch size is largely unknown in the Pacific Northwest, but brood size for 40 broods in British Columbia ranged from 1 to 4 young, with 50% having 2 young (Campbell et al. 1990).

Hunting Behavior and Diet. The Barred Owl is a nocturnal and crepuscular hunter, although some hunting does occasionally happen during the day. Hunting technique is virtually the same as used by the Spotted Owl. Very little information has been obtained on the food habits of Barred Owls in the Pacific Northwest. In Washington, 92 prey items revealed that Barred Owls fed most frequently on deer mice, northern flying squirrels, microtine voles, moles, and shrews (Hamer et al. 1989). Overall, these researchers found the Barred Owl diet to be more diverse than that of co-existing Spotted Owls. In western Montana, wintering Barred Owls fed primarily on microtine voles (Marks et al. 1984).

Territory and Density. The Barred Owl is highly territorial and defends its entire home range which is usually under a square mile in size. In Washington, the mean nearest neighbor distance between nests was 2.2 times smaller than sympatric-nesting spotted owls (Hamer et al. 1989). Overall, 30 radiotagged Barred Owls had a mean summer home range size of 538 acres (218 ha) (Hamer et al. 1989).

Survey Methods. Like its close relative the Spotted Owl, the Barred Owl can be readily surveyed by broadcasting taped calls or using vocal imitations (Bosakowski 1987). These owls are also frequently detected during systematic calling surveys for spotted owls (TB). In one study, calling inventories were conducted by driving along forest roads and stopping every 1/3 mile (540 meters) to call and listen for owls (Hamer et al. 1989). Hiking trails and unroaded areas were surveyed on foot and calls were given every few minutes.

Conservation and Management. Forsman and Bull (1989) remarked that little is known of the biology of Barred Owls in the Pacific Northwest, but they suggested retaining large snags and trees that contain cavities and retaining stands of mature trees in intensively managed forests. Expanding populations may be competing for food and habitat of the Spotted Owl and evidence of some displacement has been observed (Forsman and Bull 1989). Hybridization has occurred ("Sparred Owl") and could further reduce population viability of the threatened Spotted Owl (Hamer et al. 1994).

Barred Owls breed throughout the Washington Cascades below 4,000 feet in elevation (Wenatchee National Forest).

GREAT GREY OWL *(Strix nebulosa)*
Length 22"; Wingspan 60"

Resident Range

Great Grey Owl.

GERRIT VYN

Range. The Great Grey Owl breeds throughout the central and eastern Cascades of Washington and Oregon. Eastward it also occurs in the Blue Mountains of Oregon and Washington, and the Selkirk Mountains and Okanagon Highlands of Washington (Bull and Forsman 1989). The species breeds throughout nearly all of British Columbia, except for the southwestern coast, Vancouver Island and the Queen Charlotte Islands (Godfrey 1986). Breeding evidence has occurred at elevations of 2,950 to 4,000 feet (900 and 1,220 m) in British Columbia (Campbell et al. 1990). Great Grey Owls are generally described as non-migratory and nomadic with irregular southward and downslope migrations in winter (Duncan and Hayward 1994).

Status. The status of this forest owl is uncertain, but declines are suspected in some areas where they are under study. Bryan and Forsman (1987) suggested that the species was declining in southcentral Oregon. Elimination of nest and roost sites by commercial logging and salvage logging in lodgepole pine stands (bark beetle control) and urban sprawl have been implicated (Bryan and Forsman 1987). In Oregon it is listed as a sensitive species (Marshall 1992a).

Habitat Requirements. Great Grey Owls breed in open forest or forest with adjacent deep meadows, bogs, muskegs, or other openings (Duncan and Hayward 1994; Campbell et al. 1990). In southcentral Oregon, 61 of 63 owl locations were located adjacent to meadows and most locations (59 of 63) were associated with lodgepole pine or lodgepole and ponderosa pine, and mixed conifer associations were found in the remaining 4 sites (Bryan and Forsman 1987).

Nesting. This large owl nests in old hawk nests, on mistletoe platforms, on snags with broken tops, and on artificial nest platforms. Of 11 nests that were found in southcentral Oregon, 10 were in old platform nests built by diurnal raptors and one was in a cavity of a large snag (Bryan and Forsman 1987). In that study, the mean distance of nests to meadows was 900 feet (275 meters), live tree density averaged 238 trees per acre (587 trees per ha), and canopy cover averaged 46.5 percent. In Northeastern Oregon, another study found 46 nests, with 25 on stick platforms of Northern Goshawks, Red-tailed Hawks, or mistletoe, 11 on artificial platforms, and 10 on snags with broken tops (Bull and Henjum 1990). At these nests, canopy closure generally exceeded 60% and the percentage of forested area within a 1,640 foot (500 m) radius varied between 52 and 99%. Of six nests reported for British Columbia, 2 were in abandoned

goshawk nests in quaking aspen, 2 were in mistletoe brooms in aspens, 1 was in an old Red-tailed Hawk nest in an aspen, and 1 was in an unidentified stick nest (Campbell et al. 1990).

Eggs and Young. The eggs are plain white, less rounded, and more oval than most owl eggs (Godfrey 1986) and average about 2.1 x 1.7 inches (54.2 x 43.4 mm) in size (Bent 1938). Brood size for 21 broods in British Columbia ranged from 1 to 4 young, with 16 broods having 2 or 3 young (Campbell et al. 1990).

Roosting. Roosting typically occurs within forest stands away from the edge of openings. In summer, the owls roost in trees with fairly dense canopies and close to the trunk during inclement weather (Duncan and Hayward 1994). In winter and late spring, the owls will occasionally roost in sunny open areas and atop snags (Bull and Duncan 1993).

Hunting Behavior and Diet. Despite their large size and formidable stature, Great Greys feed almost exclusively on small rodents. In Oregon, a collection of 4,546 prey items

Great Grey Owl clutching a mouse.

revealed that voles were the principal diet of Great Grey Owls (Bull et al. 1989a). The voles included 51.6% *Microtus* and 13.9% *Clethrionomys*, and pocket gophers (*Thomomys*) accounted for 28.8% of the diet. Hunting is generally done from perches where the owls can listen and watch the ground intently for prey. The average perch to prey distance is 34.4 feet (10.5 m) (Bull and Henjum 1990). In winter, Great Grey Owls use a technique called "snow-plunging" whereby they hover a few feet above snow listening for small mammals, and then dive blindly into the snow with their feet and talons to a depth of 12 inches (30 cm) (Nero 1980). Success rates as high as 65% have been reported (Duncan 1992). Before the nesting season, most hunting is done in the late afternoon, but both daytime and nocturnal hunting are done when young are in the nest (Oeming 1955).

Territory and Density. Breeding season home ranges of this large owl are often relatively small and there is some evidence that territoriality is weak or non-existent during good prey years. In Oregon, 5 nesting pairs were found in one 716-acre (290-ha) study area and 7 pairs were found in a 2,314-acre (937-ha) area (Bull and Henjum 1987).

Average home range size in Oregon was 1,112 acres (450 ha) with a range of 321 to 1,606 acres (130 to 650 ha) and maximum distance traveled by adults from their nest averaged 8.4 miles (13.4 km) (Bull and Henjum 1990).

Survey Methods. At night, these impressive owls will respond to taped calls or vocal imitations. Bryan and Forsman (1987) used a portable taperecorder at night (10 minutes after sunset to 30 minutes before sunrise) to elicit responses of Great Grey Owls while walking transects. During the day, researchers return to areas with responses to examine old goshawk nests and broken-off tree stubs for signs of nesting by these owls.

Conservation and Management. For Oregon forests, Bryan and Forsman (1987) recommended protection of nest sites and use of artificial nest platforms to provide a consistent supply of nest sites in managed forests. Bull and Henjum (1990) erected 158 artificial platforms and found that the owls preferred higher platforms (50 vs. 30 feet), open platforms (vs. box), and platforms within stands (330-660 feet or 100-200 m) as opposed to platforms placed on forest edges.

Breeding habitat in extensive lodgepole-pine forest at Chasm Provincial Park in central British Columbia.

LONG-EARED OWL *(Asio otus)*

Length 13"; Wingspan 39"

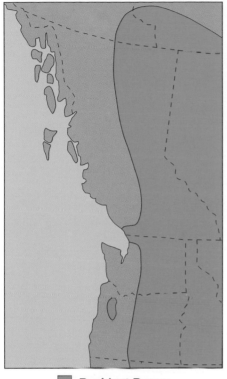

■ Resident Range

Long-eared Owl.

Range. The Long-eared Owl can be found year-round throughout Oregon and Washington (Marti and Marks 1989). Washington GAP Analysis shows few breeding sites, with most breeding limited to southeastern steppe areas (Smith et al. 1997). A few breeding sites were found in coastal northwestern counties and north-eastern open ponderosa pine forests. In Oregon, it also breeds east of the Cascade Range (Csuti et al. 1997). It also breeds in southern British Columbia (Godfrey 1986) at elevations ranging from sea level to 3,350 feet (1,020 m) (Campbell et al. 1990).

Status. Little is known about the status of the secretive Long-eared Owl in the Pacific

Northwest, but in California, some evidence of pesticide poisoning is being investigated and loss of riparian habitat (containing Corvid nests) has also been suspected (Marti and Marks 1989). Nesting by these owls has been very sporadic at Malheur NWR in southeastern Oregon with as many as 24 pairs in certain years (Littlefield 1990).

Habitat Requirements. Long-eared Owls usually nest and roost in thick groves of conifers or hardwoods (young to mid-seral stage), but typically hunt in adjacent open fields, meadows, marshes, or open woodlands (Bent 1938; Reynolds 1970). Surveys revealed that this species may be more abundant in conifer forests of Oregon than previously thought (Bull et al. 1989b). Based on prey taken, it was concluded that most hunting was occurring within forests or on the edge (Bull et al. 1989b). The species also occurs in desert habitats; nesting in old Corvid nests in riparian groves that border creeks and rivers (Marti and Marks 1989).

Nesting. The nest site can also be in a relatively small plantation, grove, shelter belt, hedgerow or riparian strip where they use old nests of hawks, crows, or magpies (Bent 1938; Call 1978; Marti and Marks 1989). In Oregon, 20 nests were found in extensive grand-fir forests (avg. 87 years old) with high canopy closure (80%), and only about 10% of the area had been logged in the past 40 years (Bull et al. 1989b). These nests averaged 105 meters (345') from openings and only 21% of the study area was considered non-forested. Average nest height was 32.1 feet (9.8 m) and 19 nests were built on mistletoe brooms and one was built in an old *Accipiter* nest. Of 61 nests in British Columbia, 92% were in stands of dense deciduous shrubs and trees including western birch (43%), willows (33%), hawthorn, black cottonwood, aspen, red alder and wild cherry, and coniferous nests were in Douglas fir, ponderosa pine, and spruce (Campbell et al. 1990). The heights of 70 tree nests ranged from 4.6 to 44.9 feet (1.4 to 13.7 m), and one nest was on the ground. Tree nests (n=75) were in old nests of Common Crow (92%), Black-billed Magpie (4%), and Northwestern Crow (4%).

Eggs and Young. The eggs are white (Godfrey 1986) and average about 1.6 x 1.3 inches in size (Herron et al. 1985) or 40 x 32.5 mm in Bent (1938). Egg dates for 66 clutches in British Columbia ranged from 16 March to 11 June, clutch size for 68 clutches ranged from 1 to 6 eggs, with 90% having 4 to 6, and brood size for 69 broods ranged from 1 to 6 young, with 71% of broods having 3 to 5 young (Campbell et al. 1990).

Hunting Behavior and Diet. Long-eared Owls depend heavily on small mammals for food, although small birds are occasionally taken. In Northeastern Oregon, these owls feed mostly on pocket gophers (55.7%), voles (22.1%), deer mice (11.8%), small birds (3.9%), shrews (3.3%) and other small vertebrates (Bull et al. 1989b). In the Okanagan Valley of southcentral British Columbia, mammals accounted for 97% of the 331 prey items found at Long-eared Owl nests (Hooper and Nyhof 1986). Meadow voles (23%), *Perognathus parvus* (19%), deer mice (15%), and other *Microtus* spp. voles (28.3%) were the dominant prey species. These owls search for prey with low, gliding flights, where they hunt open areas, and occasional wooded and forested habitat.

Roosting. In winter, these owls often roost communally in groups of 2 to 20 owls, but occasionally up to 100 owls (Marks et al. 1994). In British Columbia, the largest communal roost was 6 birds in the Okanagan (Cannings et al. 1987). Roost sites are usually in thick conifers, but dense riparian (broadleaf) trees and vine tangles are also used (Bent 1938).

Territory and Density. This extremely nocturnal owl is not strongly territorial and can breed at fairly high densities in response to periodic superabundances of small mammals. Sometimes they will even nest in loose colonies of 3 to 4 nesting pairs (Bent 1938). Although no formal density study has been done in the Pacific Northwest, Bull et al. (1989b) reported finding 20 nests over a 2-year period all within a 14,128-acre (5,720 ha) study area in northeastern Oregon. In the sagebrush-juniper ecotone of southcentral Idaho average nesting density was 0.60 pairs per square mile (1.55 pairs per square km) (Thurow and White 1984).

Survey Methods. Bull et al. (1989b) surveyed Long-eared Owls by walking routes after sunset and calling with vocal imitations every 330 feet (100 m). The routes were spaced less than 0.31 miles (500 m)

Long-eared Owl concealment pose: eyes squinted and plumage flattened to appear like a broken branch.

to ensure that the entire study area was called. To locate nests, they returned the next day to sites where owls had responded and looked for whitewash, pellets, and potential nest platforms. Call (1978) recommended driving available road systems while scanning for potential nest platforms (magpie, crow, raptors), conducting systematic searches of conifer groves, and broadcasting taped calls every quarter-mile at night. He also recommended that nests must be carefully observed because distant observations with binoculars usually will not reveal incubating or brooding birds. The owls will often sit tight on the nest and the surveyor must rap the nest tree or even the nest itself before the bird will reveal itself. Thurow and White (1984) climbed to every nest that was observed in

their study area to get a reliable estimate of nesting density.

Conservation and Management. Bull et al. (1989b) noted that all nests were in dense, unlogged stands, despite systematic searches in many habitat types. Thus, the species may not tolerate thinning or other silvicultural activities in potential nesting stands. Loss of riparian woodlands and isolated tree groves would be detrimental, but the effects of overgrazing are unknown (Marks et al. 1994). No specific management plans have been instituted for the Long-eared Owl in North America (Marti and Marks 1989). Call (1979) recommended preservation of stick nests for this species as well as other raptors.

SHORT-EARED OWL *(Asio flammeus)*
Length 13"; Wingspan 41"

Breeding Range

Resident Range

A wintering Short-eared Owl
roosts on the ground.

throughout the Willamette Valley (Csuti et al. 1997). It is a nomadic species, which is highly migratory in the northern part of its range (Holt and Leasure 1993). Spring migrants first appear during the first week of March at Malheur NWR in southern Oregon, with their peak numbers occurring between 25 March and 25 April (Littlefield 1990).

Range. The Short-eared Owl can be found year-round throughout Oregon and Washington (Marti and Marks 1989). It also ranges throughout all of British Columbia except possibly for the Queen Charlotte Islands (Godfrey 1986) and breeds locally in the south and central interior and on the mainland coast from the Fraser River Delta to Fort Langely from sea level to at least 3,200 feet (975 m) (Campbell et al. 1990). In Washington, it breeds predominantly east of the Cascade Range in open treeless terrain, but occasionally in open coastal marshes (Smith et al. 1997). In Oregon, it also breeds mostly east of the Cascade Range in open treeless country, but also occurs widely

Status. Populations of this owl have always been small and localized to special habitats, but there is evidence of decline in some areas of the Pacific Northwest. In western Washington, the species was formerly found at many sites with prairie vegetation (Jewett et al. 1953), but is apparently absent now (Smith et al. 1997). Data from BBS Routes show only a small number of National Forests with this species, but the percent annual change has declined in Washington over the period of 1980-89 (Sharp 1992). BBS routes for all of Oregon and Washington show a non-significant increase from 1966-89 (Holt and Leasure 1993). This owl is currently Blue-Listed in British Columbia.

Habitat Requirements. The Short-eared Owl is not a forest owl, but an open-country raptor of marshes, bogs, tundra, old fields, pastures, cropland, and meadows (Johnsgard 1988; Sharp 1992; Holt and Leasure 1993). Much like the Northern Harrier, it occurs in annual grasslands up to high-elevation mountain-meadow habitat. These owls are commonly found in treeless areas using large mounds, snags, and fence posts as perches and requiring dense non-woody vegetation (grasses, reeds, sedges, rushes), brush, and open wetlands for roosting and nesting.

Short-eared Owl in flight.

Nesting. The Short-eared Owl nests on the ground in a concealed patch of dense vegetation ground where they may create a small depression or "nest scrape" (Marti and Marks 1989; Holt and Leasure 1993), sparsely lined with grasses, leaves, or sometimes a few feathers (Campbell et al. 1990). In British Columbia, most nests (44%, n=36) were in shrubby, grassy fields adjacent to agriculture, while the remainder were in airport fields (7), marshes (5), open rangeland (3), sagebrush plains (3), and hayfields (3) (Campbell et al. 1990). At Malheur NWR in southeastern Oregon, their preferred nesting habitat is wild rye-shrub covered uplands surrounded by meadows and marshes (Littlefield 1990).

Eggs and Young. The eggs are white (Godfrey 1986) and average about 1.6 x 1.2 inches (40.6 x 30.4 mm) in size (Herron et al. 1985). Clutch completion has been recorded as early as 14 March at Malheur NWR in southeastern Oregon (Littlefield 1990). Egg dates for 32 clutches in British Columbia ranged from 24 March to 9 July, clutch size for 30 clutches ranged from 1 to 13 eggs, with 57% having 6 or 7 eggs, and brood size for 26 broods ranged from 1 to 8 young, with 15 broods having 5 or 6 young (Campbell et al. 1990).

Roosting. In winter, these owls often roost communally in large groups of up to 110 owls (Campbell et al. 1990), but groups of 3 to 10 are more common. These owls roost most often on the ground, but are known to roost in coniferous trees during periods of snow cover (Bosakowski 1986).

Hunting Behavior and Diet. These medium-sized owls feed primarily on voles and other small mammals, but will also feed on birds, reptiles, insects and amphibians (Earhart and Johnson 1970). In the Palouse Prairie of southeastern Washington, wintering Short-eared Owls fed primarily on voles (*Microtus montanus* and *longicaudus*; 115) and deer mice (42) (Fitzner and Fitzner 1975). Similar results were obtained from Sauvies Island west of Portland, Oregon where a sample of 81 prey remains revealed 69 voles (*Microtus* spp.), 3 deer mice, and 9 unidentified birds (Taylor 1984). These owls hunt primarily on the wing by flying low off the ground, hovering, and then swooping down on prey that are heard or seen. Breeding Short-eared Owls have foraged up to 3.5 miles from their nest (Brown 1985).

Territory and Density. Short-eared Owl communal winter roosts may become breeding sites and owls may breed locally at high densities (Holt and Leasure 1993). In Montana, 30 active nests were found in a 405-acre (164-ha) area, which yielded a density of about 1 nest per 13.6 acres (5.5 ha) (Holt and Leasure 1993). Conversely, these owls seem to maintain relatively small breeding territories. Clark (1975) found a range of 57 to 299 acres (23 to 121 ha) for breeding territory size in Manitoba.

Survey Methods. Short-eared Owls respond vigorously to taped calls during winter nights, often "buzzing" the investigators standing next to the tape player (Bosakowski 1989). Call (1978) suggested broadcasting of taped calls every quarter-mile at night, or making noise (clapping, etc.) while traversing suitable open habitats to flush owls during the day. Where driving is appropriate, the owls will usually flush about 30 to 50 yards ahead of moving vehicles. Searches for nests should be intensified in areas where courtship has been observed. Diligent foot searches or dragging ropes may be needed to reveal nest sites by flushing females, but precautions should be taken to avoid leading ground predators to nests (Tate 1997). Surveys are most successful when the owls are most active, around dawn and dusk, but sometimes in late afternoons, two to three hours before sunset. Counts of owls leaving or departing roosts in the evening have been used to estimate the size of winter communal roosts (Bosakowski 1986, 1989; Kochert 1986).

Conservation and Management. This ground-nester is dependent on dense ground cover, thus removal renders the owl vulnerable to predation (Marti and Marks 1989). This owl continues to benefit from waterfowl management (Holt and Leasure 1993), wetlands restoration, and the National Wildlife Refuge system. Intensive agriculture, overgrazing, and burning continues to cause destruction of nesting habitat in eastern Washington (Smith et al. 1997). Areas of habitat greater than 124 acres (50 ha) should be considered potential breeding or wintering habitat (Tate 1997). There is also some direct proof of pesticide contamination of owls and their eggs as well as several mortalities, but the extent of the problem is not yet known (Marti and Marks 1989). Human visits to nests may cause disturbance or increase nest losses if paths are worn leading mammalian predators to nests.

Short-eared Owl on arctic coastal plain nesting grounds near Prudhoe Bay, Alaska.

BOREAL OWL *(Aegolius funereus)*
Length 10"; Wingspan 24"

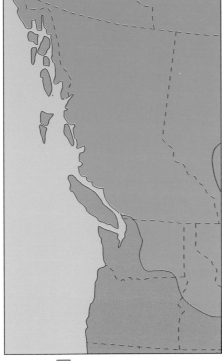

Resident Range

Boreal Owl.

JIM ZIPP

Range. The Washington GAP Analysis shows that the breeding range occurs in the Northern Cascades, Selkirk Mountains (extreme north-eastern tip of the state), and Blue Mountains, where it is seldom found below 4,000 feet (1,220 m) (Smith et al. 1997). The Blue Mountains in the northeast corner of Oregon are considered breeding range (Platt and Enderson 1989) as well the higher elevations of the northeastern slope of the Cascades (Csuti et al. 1997). In British Columbia, the northern half of the province is considered breeding range with a southward extension into the higher elevations of the Rocky Mountains (Godfrey 1986).

Status. This small owl is considered uncommon to rare in appropriate habitat in Washington, but may be more common than believed (Smith et al. 1997). It is considered rare in British Columbia where only three breeding records have been established (Campbell et al. 1990).

Habitat Requirements. Boreal Owls inhabit boreal and subalpine forests most often in spruce-fir types, followed by lodgepole pine, mixed-conifer, Douglas fir, aspen, black spruce, red-fir, and western hemlock (Hayward 1994). Nesting sites were located in older, more complex forest with larger trees, higher basal area, and reduced understory development than available habitat (Hayward 1994).

Nesting. The Boreal Owl is an obligate cavity-nester, primarily relying on the presence of old woodpecker holes (Pileated Woodpeckers and Northern Flickers) for nesting cavities. In Idaho, nest cavities were in live trees or snags with an average diameter of 25 inches (64 cm) (Hayward et al. 1993). Only one nest site is known from British Columbia, a single infertile Boreal Owl egg was reported from a nest box at Rabbit Lake, near Okanagan Falls (Campbell et al. 1990).

Eggs and Young. Clutch size is typically 3 to 7, usually 4 to 6, and the eggs are white, averaging 1.3 x 1.1 inches (32.3 x 26.9 mm) in size (Bent 1938). Productivity for six nests in Idaho was 2.3 fledglings per successful nest (Hayward 1989).

Hunting Behavior and Diet. Boreal Owls are strongly nocturnal and hunt exclusively by perch hunting (Hayward 1994). The hunting style is very active as the owls move frequently from perch to perch, usually flying 30 to 100 feet (10 to 30 m) between perches (Hayward 1994). Small mammals made-up the bulk of the diet in Idaho (voles, pocket gophers, shrews, and mice), with the remainder comprised of insects (13%) and birds (5%) (Hayward et al. 1993).

Territory and Density. For a small owl, the Boreal has a rather large home range. Summertime home ranges averaged 2,919 acres (1,182 ha) in central Idaho while wintertime home ranges were even larger, averaging 3,584 acres (1,451 ha) (Hayward 1994). No reliable estimates of nesting density are known for the Pacific Northwest.

Survey Methods. Due to their preference for high, remote forests and their strictly nocturnal habits, these owls are indeed difficult to detect. Night surveys using broadcasts of taped calls is probably the most effective way of locating territorial owls. Whelton (1989) conducted 21 night hiking surveys in Washington and Oregon where he played tape recordings for about 5 minutes at 200 meter (656 feet) intervals, and 16 driving routes were also established on National Forests logging roads. To locate nests, surveyors can return during the day to sites where owls responded and look for whitewash, pellets, and potential nesting cavities.

Conservation and Management. Maintenance of forested landscapes is a prime requirement for Boreal Owl conservation. In particular, silvicultural prescriptions must provide for retention of large-diameter trees over space and time with mature and older forest well-represented in the landscape (Hayward 1994). Clearcutting was not advised for Boreal Owl habitats, but other silvicultural management (e.g., selection harvest) may be possible if it maintains canopy structure and forest floor moisture (Hayward 1994).

High-elevation coniferous forests of the Canadian Rockies in eastern British Columbia can harbor species such as the Boreal Owl.

NORTHERN SAW-WHET OWL *(Aegolius acadicus)*
Length 7"; Wingspan 17"

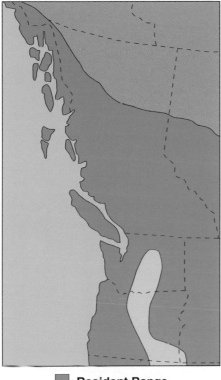

Resident Range

Wintering Range

Range. In Washington, Gabrielson and Jewett (1970) considered the Northern Saw-whet Owl as a fairly common and local permanent resident throughout the region where it occurs in all forest types (Smith et al. 1997). Its distribution is more local in the upper Columbia River basin where it is mostly limited to riparian vegetation (Smith et al. 1997). In Oregon, it breeds throughout coniferous forest regions of the Cascade, Coast, and Blue Mountains (Csuti et al. 1997). It is a permanent resident across southern Canada, including the southern half of the British Columbia mainland, Vancouver Island and the Queen Charlotte Islands (Godfrey 1986) from sea level to 4,000 feet (1,220 m) in elevation (Campbell

et al. 1990). Some individuals remain to winter in the general area of their breeding range but others may wander southward (Godfrey 1986).

Status. The Saw-whet Owl is quiet and retiring in its nesting habits, hence its population and breeding status are not as completely known as many of the other species of raptors. The *brooksi* subspecies is currently Blue-Listed in British Columbia.

Habitat Requirements. This small owl is noted for its adaptability in habitat selection. It is known to breed, forage, and roost in coniferous and mixed woodlands and also in riparian woodlands along streams or around lakes or wetlands of dense alder thickets. It may be somewhat more common in dense conifer woodlands and plantations, wooded swamps, and bogs. In the Okanagan Valley of southern British Columbia, Saw-whet Owls breed in montane coniferous forest and riparian deciduous woodlands (Cannings 1987) and were most common from 1,640 to 3,280 feet (500 to 1,000 m) in elevation, although they may be found up to 4,600 feet (1,400 m) before apparently being replaced by the Boreal Owl.

Nest Sites. Typical nests in the Pacific Northwest include old woodpecker holes, old squirrel nests, or tree hollows (Gabrielson and Jewett 1970). Of 12 nests located by Cannings (1987) in southern British Columbia, 10 were in nest boxes placed at 8.5 to 20 feet (2.6 to 6.1 m) above ground and two were in northern flicker holes in ponderosa pine snags at 9.2 to 15.1 feet (2.8 to 4.6 m) in height. Overall, a total of 31 nests have been reported in British Columbia with 20 in natural cavities in coniferous and deciduous trees and 11 nests in nest boxes (Campbell et al. 1990).

Heights of 21 tree nests ranged from 5.9 to 45 feet (1.8 to 13.7 m) and 17 nests were in woodpecker holes and 3 were in natural cavities (Campbell et al. 1990). A nest date at Yakima in Washington was April 12, but immatures were observed in early August at Owyhigh Lakes and early September at St. Andrews Park (Gabrielson and Jewett 1970).

Eggs and Young. The eggs are white (Godfrey 1986) and average about 1.2 x 1.0 inches (30.5 x 25.4 mm) in size (Herron et al. 1985). Egg dates for 27 clutches in British Columbia ranged from 7 April to 17 August, clutch size for 26 clutches ranged from 3 to 7 eggs, with 65% having 5 or 6 eggs, and brood size for 47 broods ranged from 1 to 6 young, with 51% having 2 to 4 young (Campbell et al. 1990). Cannings (1987) noted that nests might be abandoned following disturbance, but females often initiate a second clutch in another nest site.

Roosting. These tiny, compact owls roost in a wide variety of places including dense vegetation, tree cavities, and man-made structures. Ten of 13 roost sites in Oregon were in dense, low thickets of sapling grand fir or western larch sapling layers beneath old-growth ponderosa pine (Boule 1982). In Washington, roost sites bordering the east-side of the Columbia River were located in orchards and orchard windbreaks, and river-side thickets of willow interspersed with Russian olive and Siberian elm. Conifers, especially Douglas firs were almost exclusively chosen if present (Groves 1985). Perch heights of 23 roost sites ranged from 4.6 to 16.4 feet (1.4 to 5.0 m) above ground in trees that are 26.2 to 32.8 feet (8 to 10 m) in height (Groves 1985). In British Columbia, dense tangles, natural cavities, and man-made structures are used for roosting, including garages, carports, greenhouses, barns, stables, cabins, airport hangers, and even metal garbage cans (Campbell et al. 1990).

Northern Saw-whet Owl.

Hunting Behavior and Diet. Food of Saw-whet Owls seems to center on small rodents, especially mice, voles, and shrews, but bats, young squirrels, birds, and insects may also be occasionally preyed upon (Cannings 1993; Godfrey 1986). Winter food of Saw-whets in north-central Washington consisted mostly of small mammals, especially meadow voles (*Microtus* spp.) and deer mice along with small numbers of birds (Grove 1985). Prey remains found in 57 pellets collected in old-growth conifer forests in the Wallowa-Whitman National Forest in Oregon contained mostly deer mice which comprised over 75 percent of the total prey followed by small numbers of other rodents, and a single passerine bird (Boule 1982). Prey remains found at nests and roosts in southern British Columbia consisted mostly of deer mice (84.4%) followed by small numbers of other rodents, shrews, and birds in pine-fir forests, but in deciduous woodlands, Great Basin pocket mice and voles (*Microtus* spp.) were also important (Cannings 1987). Prey is normally captured on the ground after pouncing from a low-elevated perch site.

Territory and Density. Territories are proclaimed and established through vocalizations. Breeding densities in southern British Columbia, based on singing male counts, averaged 0.32 per mile (0.2 owls per km) in pine-fir forests and 0.8 owls per mile (0.5 per km) in deciduous woodland habitat (Cannings 1987). Sizes of home ranges occupied by two nesting males were 351 and 393 acres (142 and 159 ha) based on radio tracking (Cannings 1987).

Survey Methods. While playback of tape recorded calls has facilitated winter and breeding surveys of this species, the location of nests and information on nesting data is difficult to obtain as most nests are located fortuitously or by telemetry of captured and released individuals.

Conservation and Management. Winter mortality of Northern Saw-whet Owls may be a problem, especially during severe winters with comparatively long periods of cold and deep snows as this small owl has difficulty securing small mammal prey in their subnivean environment (Godfrey 1986). Year-round habitat needs include suitable roost sites; sapling thickets beneath old-growth are important and should be retained in any forest management practices. Conversely, Boule (1982) noted that sapling thickets were uncommon in managed forests and identified, this, plus the declining mature timber may pose a habitat loss to this small owl in Oregon.

Lakeside forest habitat: Tatla Lake in west-central British Columbia.

REFERENCES

A

Allen, H. A. 1991. Status and management of the Peregrine Falcon in Washington. Pages 72-74 in: (Pagel, J.E., ed.) Proceedings, Symposium on Peregrine Falcons in the Pacific Northwest; 16-17 January 1991, Ashland, OR. Rogue River National Forest, Medford, OR.

Anderson, B., J. Frost, K. McAllister, D. Pinco and P. Crocker-Davis. 1986. Bald Eagles in Washington. *Washington Wildlife* 36:13-20.

Anderson, R.J. and A.M. Bruce. 1980. A comparison of selected Bald and Golden Eagle nests in western Washington. Pages 117-120 in: (Knight, R.L., ed.) Proceedings of the Washington Bald Eagle Symposium, Seattle, WA.

Anthony, R.G. and F.B. Isaacs. 1989. Characteristics of Bald Eagle nests in Oregon. *Journal of Wildlife Management* 53:148-159.

Anthony, R.G., R.L. Knight, G.T. Allen, B.R. McClelland and J.I. Hodges. 1982. Habitat use by nesting and roosting Bald Eagles in the Pacific Northwest. Trans. North Am. Wildl. Nat. Resour. Conf. 47:332-342.

Anthony, R.G., M.G. Garrett, and F.B. Isaacs. 1999. Double-survey estimates of Bald Eagle populations in Oregon. *Journal of Wildlife Management* 63:794-802.

Austin, K.K. 1992. Habitat use and home range size of breeding northern goshawks in the southern Cascades. M.S. Thesis, Oregon State University, Corvallis. 57 pp.

Balding, T. and E. Dibble. 1984. Responses of Red-tailed Hawk, Red-shouldered Hawk, and Broad-winged Hawks to high-volume playback recordings. Passenger Pigeon 46:71-75.

B

Balgooyen, T.G. 1969. Pygmy owl attacks California Quail. Auk 86:358.

Bart, J. and E.D. Forsman. 1992. Dependence of Northern Spotted Owls *Strix occidentalis caurina* on old-growth forests in the western USA. Biological Conservation 62:95-100.

Bechard, M.J., R.L. Knight, D.G. Smith, and R.E. Fitzner. 1990. Nest sites and habitats of sympatric hawks (*Buteo* spp.) in Washington. *Journal of Field Ornithology* 61:159-170.

Bechard, M. J., and J. K. Schumtz. 1995. Ferruginous Hawk (*Buteo regalis*). The Birds of North America, No 172. The Academy of Natural Sciences of Philadelphia. Philadelphia, PA.

Bednarz, J.C. and J.J. Dinsmore. 1982. Nest-sites and habitat of Red-shouldered and Red-tailed Hawks in Iowa. Wilson Bull. 94:31-45.

Bednarz, J.C., D. Klem, Jr., L.J. Goodrich, and S.E. Senner. 1990. Migration counts of raptors at Hawk Mountain, Pennsylvania, as indicators of population trends, 1934-1986. Auk 107: 96-109.

Beebe, F.L. 1960. The marine Peregrines of the Northwest Pacific coast. Condor 62:145-189.

Beecham, J.J. and M.N. Kochert. 1975. Breeding biology of the Golden Eagle in southwestern Idaho. Wilson Bull. 87:506-513.

Bent, A.C. 1937. Life histories of North American birds of prey. Part I. U.S. National Museum Bulletin No. 167.

Bent, A.C. 1938. Life histories of North American birds of prey. Part 2. U.S. National Museum Bulletin No. 170.

Bevis, K.R., J.E. Richards, G.M. King, and E.E. Hanson. 1997. Food habits of the Northern Spotted Owl (*Strix occidentalis caurina*) at six nest sites in Washington's East Cascades. Pages 68-73 in: (Duncan, J.R., D.H. Johnson, and T.H. Nicholls, eds.) Biology and conservation of owls of the northern hemisphere. USDA Forest Service, Gen. Tech. Report NC-190.

Bloom, P.H. 1983. Notes on the distribution and biology of Flammulated Owl in California. Western Birds 14: 49-52.

Bloom, P.H. 1985. Raptor movements in California. Pages 313-323 in: (M. Harwood, ed.) Proceedings of Hawk Migration Conference IV, Rochester, NY.

Bloom, P.H., and S. J. Hawks. 1982. Food habits of nesting Golden Eagles in north eastern California and northwest Nevada. Raptor Research 16: 110-115.

Bloom, P.H. and M.D. McCrary. 1996. The urban *buteo*: Red-shouldered Hawks in southern California. Pages 31-39 in: (D.M. Bird, D.E. Varland, and J.J. Negro, eds.) Raptors in human landscapes: adaptations to built and cultivated environments. 396 pp.

Bloom, P.H., G.R. Stewart, and B.J. Walton. 1986. The status of the Northern Goshawk in California, 1981-1983. Administrative Report 85-1, California Department of Fish and Game, Sacramento.

Bloom, P.H., M.D. McCrary, and M.J. Gibson. 1993. Red-shouldered Hawk home-range and habitat use in southern California. J. Wildl. Manage. 57:258-265.

Bolsinger, C.L. and K.L. Waddell. 1993. Area of old-growth forests in California, Oregon, and Washington. Resource Bulletin PNW-RB-197, USDA Forest Service, Pacific Northwest Research Station, Portland, OR. 26 pp.

Bosakowski, T. 1986. Short-eared Owl winter roosting strategies. *American Birds* 40:237-240.

Bosakowski, T. 1987. Census of Barred and Spotted Owls. Pages: 307-308. In. Proceedings, Biology and Conservation of Northern Forest Owls. Winnipeg, Manitoba. USDA Forest Service General Technical Report RM-142.

Bosakowski, T. 1989. Observations on the evening departure and activity of wintering Short-eared Owls in New Jersey. J. Raptor Research 23:162-166.

Bosakowski, T. 1997. Breeding bird abundance and habitat relationships on a private industrial forest in the western Washington Cascades. *Northwest Science* 71:244-253.

Bosakowski, T. 1999. *The Northern Goshawk: Ecology, Behavior, and Management in North America*. Hancock House Publishers, Blaine, WA. 80 pp.

Bosakowski, T. and J. Rithaler. 1997. Goshawk and raptor inventory in the Cariboo, 1996. Prepared by Beak Pacific Ltd., Vancouver, B.C. for B.C. Environment, Ministry of Environment, Lands, and Parks, Williams Lake, B.C.

Bosakowski, T. and D.G. Smith. 1992. Comparative diets of sympatric nesting raptors in the eastern deciduous forest biome. *Canadian Journal of Zoology* 70:984-992.

Bosakowski, T. and D.G. Smith. 1998. Response of a forest raptor community to broadcasts of heterospecific and conspecific calls during the breeding season. *Canadian Field-Naturalist* 112:198-203.

Bosakowski, T. and M.E. Vaughn. 1996. Developing a practical method for surveying Northern Goshawks in managed forests of the Western Washington Cascades. *Western Journal of Applied Forestry* 11:109-113.

Bosakowski, T., R.D. Ramsey, and D.G. Smith. 1996. Habitat and spatial relationships of nesting Swainson's and Red-tailed Hawks in northern Utah. *Great Basin Naturalist* 56:341-347.

Bosakowski, T., B. McCullough, F.J. Lapsansky, and M.E. Vaughn. 1999. Northern Goshawks nesting on a private industrial forest in Western Washington. J. Raptor Research 33:240-244.

Boule, K. M. 1982. Food habits and roost-sites of Northern Saw-whet Owls in northeastern Oregon. Murrelet 63: 92-93.

Boxall, P.C. and M.R. Lein. 1982a. Territoriality and habitat selection of female Snowy Owls (*Nyctea scandiaca*) in winter. Can. J. Zool. 60:2344-2350.

Boxall, P.C. and M.R. Lein. 1982b. Feeding ecology of Snowy Owls (*Nyctea scandiaca*) in wintering in southern Alberta. Arctic 35:282-290.

Boxall, P.C. and P.H. Stepney. 1982. The distribution and status of the Barred Owl in Alberta. *Canadian Field-Naturalist* 96:46-50.

Brown, E. R. (tech. ed.) 1985. Management of wildlife and fish habitats in forests of western Oregon and Washington. USDA Forest Service R6-F&WL-192, Pacific Northwest Region, Portland, OR. 332 pp.

Brown, W.H. 1971. Winter population trends in the Red-shouldered Hawk. *American Birds* 25:813-817.

Brown, L.H. and D. Amadon. 1968. *Eagles, Hawks and Falcons of the world.* 2 Vols. McGraw-Hill, New York, NY.

Bruce, A.M., R.J. Anderson, and G.T. Allen. 1982. Observations of Golden Eagles in Western Washington. Raptor Research 16:132-134.

Bryan, T. and E.D. Forsman. 1987. Distribution, abundance, and habitat of Great Grey Owls in southcentral Oregon. Murrelet 68:45-49.

Buchanan, J.B., L.L. Irwin, and E.L. McCutchen. 1993. Characteristics of Spotted Owl nest trees in the Wenatchee National Forest. *Journal of Raptor Research* 27:1-7.

Bull, E. L., and R. G. Anderson. 1978. Notes on Flammulated Owls in northeastern Oregon. *Murrelet* 59: 26-28.

Bull, E. L. and H.A. Akenson. 1985. Common Barn Owl diet in northeastern Oregon. *Murrelet* 66:65-68.

Bull, E. L. and J. R. Duncan. 1993. Great Grey Owl (*Strix nebulosa*). The Birds of North America, No. 41. The Academy of Natural Sciences of Philadelphia, PA.

Bull, E.L. and M.G. Henjum. 1990. Ecology of the Great Grey Owl. USDA Forest Service, Gen. Tech. Report PNW-GTR-265.

Bull, E.L. and J.E. Hohmann. 1994. Breeding biology of Northern Goshawks in northeastern Oregon. Studies in Avian Biology 16:103-105.

Bull, E. L., J. E. Hohmann, and M. G. Henjum. 1987. Northern Pygmy Owl nests in northeastern Oregon. *Journal of Raptor Research* 21: 77-78.

Bull, E.L, M.G. Henjum, and R.S.

Rohweder. 1989a. Diet and optimal for aging of Great Grey Owls. *Journal of Wildlife Management* 53:47-50.

Bull, E.L., A.L. Wright, and M.G. Henjum. 1989b. Nesting and diet of Long-eared Owls in conifer forests, Oregon. Condor 91:908-912.

Bull, E. L., A. L. Wright, and M. G. Henjum. 1990. Nesting habitat of Flammulated Owls in Oregon. *Journal of Raptor Research* 24: 52-55.

C

Cade, T.J. 1960. Ecology of the Peregrine and Gyrfalcon population in Alaska. University of California Publications in Zoology 63:151-290.

Cade, T.J. 1982. *The Falcons of the World.* Cornell Univ. Press, Ithaca, NY. 144 pp.

Cade, T.J., J.H. Enderson, L.F. Kiff, and C.M. White. 1997. Are there enough good data to justify de-listing the American Peregrine Falcon? *Wildlife Society Bulletin* 25:730-738.

Cade, T.J., J.H. Enderson, C.G. Thelander, and C.M. White, (eds). 1988. Peregrine Falcon populations—their management and recovery. The Peregrine Fund, Inc. Boise, Idaho.

Cade, T.J., M. Martell, P. Redig, G. Septon, and H. Tordoff. 1996. Peregrine Falcons in urban North America. Pages 3-13 in: (D.M. Bird, D.E. Varland, and J.J. Negro, eds.) Raptors in human landscapes: adaptations to built and cultivated environments. 396 pp.

Call, M.W. 1978. Nesting habitats and surveying techniques for common western raptors. USDI, BLM Technical Note TN-316.

Call, M.W. 1979. Habitat management guides for birds of prey. USDI, BLM Technical Note TN-338. DSC, Federal Center Building 50, Denver, CO.

Campbell, R. W., and MacColl. 1978. Winter foods of Snowy Owls in south western British Columbia. *Journal of Wildlife Management* 42: 190-192.

Campbell, R.W., N.K. Dawe, I. McTaggart-

Cowan, J.M. Cooper, G.W. Kaiser, and M.C.E. McNall. 1990. *The Birds of British Columbia*. Volume 2. UBC Press, Vancouver, BC.

Cannings, R.J., and S. R. Cannings. 1982. A Flammulated Owl nest in a box. *Murrelet* 63: 66-68.

Cannings, R.J. 1987. The breeding biology of Northern Saw-whet Owls in southern British Columbia. Pages 193-198 in: Symposium Proceedings Biology and Conservation of Northern Forest Owls. USDA Forest Service General Technical Report RM-142. 319 pp.

Cannings, R.J. 1993. Northern Saw-whet Owl (*Aegolius acadicus*). *The Birds of North America*, No. 42. The Academy of Natural Sciences of Philadelphia. 20 pp.

Cannings, R. A., R. J. Cannings, and S. G. Cannings. 1987. *Birds of the Okanagan Valley, British Columbia*. Royal British Columbia Museum. Victoria, British Columbia. 420 pp.

Carey, A.B., J.A. Reid and S.P. Horton. 1990. Spotted Owl home range and habitat use in southern Oregon coast ranges. *Journal of Wildlife Management* 54:11-17.

Carey, A.B., S.P. Horton and B.L. Biswell. 1992. Northern Spotted Owls: influence of prey base and landscape character. *Ecology* 62:223-250.

Christiansen, D.A., Jr. and S.E. Reinert. 1990. Habitat use of the Northern Harrier in a coastal Massachusetts shrubland with notes on population trends in southeastern New England. *Journal of Raptor Research* 24:84-90.

Clark, R.J. 1975. A field study of the Short-eared Owl (*Asio flammeus* Pontoppidan) in North America. *Wildlife Monographs* 47:1-67.

Clark, W.S. and C.M. Anderson. 1984. First specimen record of the Broad-winged Hawk for Washington. *Murrelet* 65:93-94.

Clum, N. J., and T. J. Cade. 1994. Gyrfalcon (*Falco rusticolus*). The Birds of North America, No. 114. The Academy of Natural Sciences of Philadelphia. Philadelphia, PA. 28 pp.

Coleman, J. S., and J. D. Fraser. 1989. Habitat use and home ranges of Black and Turkey vultures. *Journal of Wildlife Management* 53: 782-792.

Colvin, B. A. 1985. Common Barn-Owl population decline in Ohio and relationship to agricultural trends. *Journal of Field Ornithology* 56: 224-235.

Colvin, B. A., P. L. Hegdal, and W. B. Jackson. 1984. A comprehensive approach to research and management of Common Barn-Owl populations. Pages 270-282 in: (W. Comb, ed.) Proceedings of the Workshop on Management of Nongame Species and Ecological Communities. Univ. Kentucky. Lexington, Kentucky.

Craighead, J.J. and F.C. Craighead, Jr. 1956. *Hawks, Owls and Wildlife*. Stackpole Publ. Co., Harrisburg, PA.

Crocker-Bedford, D.C. 1990. Goshawk reproduction and forest management. *Wildlife Society Bulletin* 18:262-269.

Crocoll, S.T. 1994. Red-shouldered Hawk (*Buteo lineatus*). The Birds of North America, No. 7. The Academy of Natural Sciences of Philadelphia, PA.

Csuti, B., A.J. Kimerling, T.A. O'neil, M.M. Shaughnessy, E.P. Gaines, and M.P. Huso. 1997. *Atlas of Oregon Wildlife: Distribution, Habitat, and Natural History*. Oregon State University Press, Corvallis, Oregon. 492 pp.

D

Daw, S.K., S. DeStefano, and R.J. Steidl. 1998. Does survey method bias the description of Northern Goshawk nest-site structure? *Journal of Wildlife Management* 62:1379-1384.

Dekker, D. 1995. Prey capture by Peregrine Falcons wintering on southern Vancouver Island, British Columbia. *J. Raptor Research* 29:26-29.

Dekker, D. and L. Bogaert, 1997. Over-ocean hunting by Peregrine Falcons in British Columbia. *J. Raptor Research* 31:381-383.

DellaSala, D.A., C.L. Thomas and R.G. Anthony. 1989. Use of domestic sheep carrion by Bald Eagles wintering in the Willamette Valley, Oregon. *Northwest Science* 63:104-108.

DeStefano, S. and J.McCloskey. 1997. Does forest structure limit the distribution of Northern Goshawks in the Coast Ranges of Oregon? *Journal of Raptor Research* 31:34-39.

DeStefano, S., S.K. Daw, S.M. Desimone, and E.C. Meslow. 1994. Density and productivity of Northern Goshawks: implications for monitoring and management. *Studies in Avian Biology* 16:88-91.

DeWeese, L.R., R.E. Pillmore, and M.L. Richmond. 1975. A device for inspecting nest cavities. *Bird Banding* 46:162-165.

Doak, D. 1989. Spotted Owls and the old-growth logging in the Pacific Northwest. *Conservation Biology* 3:389-396.

Dobler, F. C. 1993. Wintering Peregrine Falcon (*Falco peregrinus*) habitat utilization near Sequim, Washington. *Northwest Sci.* 67:231-237.

Downes, C. M., and B. T. Collins. 1996. The Canadian breeding bird survey, 1966-94. Can. Wildl. Serv. Prog. Note 210:1-36.

Duncan, J.R. 1992. Influence of prey abun dance and snow cover on Great Grey Owl breeding dispersal. Dissertation. Univ. of Manitoba, Winnipeg, Manitoba, Canada.

Duncan, J.R. and P.A. Duncan. 1998. Northern Hawk-Owl (*Surnia ulula*). The Birds of North America, No. 356. The Academy of Natural Sciences of Philadelphia, PA.

Duncan, J.R. and P.H. Hayward. 1994. Review of technical knowledge: Great Grey Owls. Pages 159-175 in: (G.D. Hayward and J. Verner, eds.) Flammulated, Boreal, and Great Grey Owls in the United States: A technical conservation assessment. USDA Forest Service, Rocky Mountain Forest and Range Experiment Station, Gen. Tech. Rep. RM-253.

Dunk, J.R. 1995. White-tailed Kite. *The Birds of North America*, No. 178. The Academy of Natural Sciences of Philadelphia, PA. 23 pp.

E

Earhart, C.M. and N.K. Johnson. 1970. Size dimorphism and food habits of North American owls. *Condor* 72:251-64.

Ehrlich, P. R., D. S. Dobkin, and D. Wheye. 1988. *The Birder's Handbook: A Field Guide to the Natural History of North American Birds*. Simon & Schuster, New York.

Ellis, D.H. 1976. First breeding records of Merlins in Montana. Condor 78:112-114.

England, A.S., M.J. Bechard, and C. S. Houston. 1997. Swainson's Hawk. *The Birds of North America*, No. 265. The Academy of Natural Sciences of Philadelphia, PA.

Erichsen, A.L., K.S. Smallwood, A.M. Commandotore, B.W. Wilson, and D.M. Fry. 1996. White-tailed Kite movement and nesting patterns in an agricultural landscape. Pages 165-176 in: (D.M. Bird, D.E. Varland, and J.J. Negro, eds.) Raptors in Human Landscapes: Adaptations to Built and Cultivated Environments. 396 pp.

F

FEMAT (Forest Ecosystem Management Assessment Team). 1993. Forest ecosystem management: an ecological, economic, and social assessment. Report of the Forest Ecosystem Management Assessment Team. U.S. Government Printing Office, Washington, D.C.

Federal Register. 1999. Endangered and threatened wildlife and plant: final rule to remove the American Peregrine Falcon from the federal list of endangered and threatened wildlife, and to remove the similarity of appearance provision for free-flying peregrines in the conterminous United States. Federal Register 64:46541-46558.

Fielder, P.C. and R.G. Starkey. 1980. Wintering Bald Eagles use along the upper Columbia River, Washington. Pages 177-193 in: (R.L. Knight, G.T. Allen, M.V. Stalmaster and C.W. Serveen, eds.) Proceedings of the Washington Bald Eagle Symposium, The Nature Conservancy, Seattle, WA.

Fischer, D. L. 1986. Daily activity patterns and habitat use of coexisting *Accipiter* Hawks in Utah. Ph.D. Thesis, Brigham Young Univ., Provo, UT.

Fitzner, R.E. 1978. The ecology and behavior of the Swainson's Hawk (*Buteo swainsoni*) in southeastern Washington. Ph.D. Diss., Washington State Univ., Pullman.

Fitzner, R.E. 1980. Behavioral ecology of the Swainson's Hawk (*Buteo swainsoni*) in Washington. Pacific Northwest Lab. PLN-2754.

Fitzner, R. E., S. G. Weiss, and J. A. Stegen. 1992. Biological assessment for threatened and endangered wildlife species, related to CERCLA characterization activities. WHC-EP-0513/UC-630. Westinghouse Hanford Company, Richland, Washington.

Fitzner, R.E. and J.N. Fitzner. 1975. Winter food habits of Short-eared Owls in the Palouse Prairie. *Murrelet* 56:2-4.

Fleming, T.L. 1987. Northern Goshawk status and habitat associations in western Washington with special emphasis on the Olympic Peninsula. Unpublished report for USDA Forest Service, Pacific Northwest Forest and Range Experiment Station, Olympia, WA.

Forsman, E.D. and A.R. Giese. 1997. Nests of Northern Spotted Owls on the Olympic Peninsula, Washington. Wilson Bull. 109:28-41.

Forsman, E.D., E.C. Meslow and M.J. Strub. 1977. Spotted Owl abundance in young versus old-growth forests, Oregon. *Wildlife Society Bulletin* 5:43-47.

Forsman, E.D., E.C. Meslow, and H.M. Wight. 1984. Distribution and biology of the Spotted Owl in Oregon. *Wildlife Monographs* 87:1-64.

Forsman, E.D., C.R. Bruce, M.A. Walter, and E.C. Meslow. 1987. A current assessment of the Spotted Owl population in Oregon. *Murrelet* 68:51-54.

Forsman, E.D., I.A. Otto, S.G. Sovern, M. Taylor, D.W. Hays, H. Allen, S.L. Roberts, and D.E. Seaman. 2001. Spatial and temporal variation in diets of Spotted Owls in Washington. J. *Raptor Research* 35:141-150.

Fox, G.A. 1964. Notes on the western race of the Pigeon Hawk. *Blue Jay* 22:140-147.

Franklin, A.B., J.P. Ward, R.J. Gutierruz, and G.I. Gould, Jr. 1990. Density of Northern Spotted Owls in Northwest California. *Journal of Wildlife Management* 54:1-10.

Franklin, J. F., K. Cromack Jr., W. Denison, A. McKee, C. Maser, J. Sedell, F. Swanson and G. Juday. 1981. Ecological characteristics of old-growth Douglas-fir forest. USDA Forest Service Gen. Tech. Rep. PNW-118, Portland, OR. 48 pp.

Frenzel, R.W. 1984. Ecology and environmental contaminants of Bald Eagles in southcentral Oregon. Ph.D. Dissertation, Oregon State University, Corvallis.

Frenzel, R.W. and R.G. Anthony. 1989. Relationship of diets and environmental contaminants in wintering Bald Eagles. *Journal of Wildlife Management* 53:792-802.

Fuller, M.R. and J.A. Mosher. 1987. Raptor survey techniques. In. *Raptor Management Techniques Manual* (Eds. B.A. Millsap and K.W. Kline), Vol. 1, National Wildlife Federation, Washington, D.C.

G

Gabrielson, I, and S. G. Jewett. 1940. *Birds of Oregon*. Oregon State University Press, Corvallis, Oregon.

Gabrielson, I. and S. G. Jewett. 1970. *Birds of the Pacific Northwest*. Dover Publications, Inc. New York, New York. 650 pp.

Gende, S.M. M.F. Wilson, B.H. Marston, M. Jacobsen, and W.P. Smith. 1998. Bald Eagle nesting density and success in relation to distance from clearcut logging in southeast Alaska. *Biological Conservation* 83:121-126.

Gilligan, J., M. Smith, D. Rogers, and A. Contreras. 1994. *Birds of Oregon*: status and distribution. Cinclus Publ., McMinnville, OR.

Godfrey, W.E. 1986. *The Birds of Canada*. revised edition, National Museums of Canada, Ottawa, Ontario. 595pp.

Goggans, R. 1985. Habitat use by Flammulated Owls in northeastern Oregon. M. S. Thesis. Oregon State University, Corvallis. 54 pp.

Goodrich, L.J., S.T. Crocoll, and S.E. Senner. 1996. Broad-winged Hawk. The *Birds of North America*, No. 218. The Academy of Natural Sciences of Philadelphia, PA. 28 pp.

Green, G.A. 1983. Ecology of breeding Burrowing Owls in the Columbia Basin, Oregon. M.S. Thesis, Oregon State University, Corvallis.

Green, G.A. and M.L. Morrison. 1983. Nest-site characteristics of sympatric Ferruginous and Swainson's Hawks. *Murrelet* 64:20-22.

Grossman, M.L. and J. Hamlet. 1964. *Birds of Prey of the World*. C.N. Potter, New York, NY. 496 pp.

Grier, J.W. 1982. Ban of DDT and subsequent recovery of reproduction in Bald Eagles. *Science* 218:1232-1235.

Grove, R. A. 1985. Northern Saw-whet Owl winter food and roosting habits in north-central Washington. *Murrelet* 66: 21-22.

Grubb, T.G. 1976. A survey and analysis of bald eagle nesting in western Washington. M.S. Thesis, University of Washington, Seattle. 87 pp.

Grubb, T.G. 1980. An evaluation of Bald Eagle nesting in western Washington. Pages 87-103 in: (R.L. Knight et al., eds.) Proceedings, Washington Bald Eagle Symposium. The Nature Conservancy, Seattle, WA.

H

Hall, P.A. 1984. Characterization of nesting habitat of goshawks (*Accipiter gentilis*) in northwestern California. M.S. Thesis, Humboldt State University, Arcata, CA.

Hamer, T.E., E.D. Forsman and M.L. Walters. 1994. Hybridization between Barred and Spotted Owls. *Auk* 111:487-492.

Hamer, T.E., S.G. Seim, and K.R. Dixon. 1989. Northern Spotted Owl and Northern Barred Owl habitat use and home range size in Washington. Preliminary Report (unpublished). Washington Dept. of Wildlife, Olympia, WA.

Hansen, A.J., M.V. Stalmaster and J.R. Newman. 1980. Habitat characteristics, function and destruction of Bald Eagle communal roosts in western Washington. Pages 221-229 in: (R.L. Knight, G.T. Allen, M.V. Stalmaster and C.W. Serveen, eds.) Proceedings of the Washington Bald Eagle symposium, The Nature Conservancy, Seattle, WA.

Hardy, G.A. 1957. Notes on the flora and fauna of Blenkinsop Lake area on southern Vancouver Island, British Columbia. Pages25-66 in: Provincial Museum of Natural History and Anthropology Report for the Year 1956, Victoria, British Columbia.

Hargis, C.D., C. McCarthy, and R.D. Perloff. 1994. Home ranges and habitats of Northern Goshawks in Eastern California. *Studies in Avian Biology* 16:66-74.

Harlow, D.L. and P.H. Bloom. 1989. *Buteos* and Golden Eagle. Pages 102-117 in: Proc. West. Raptor Manage. Symp. and Workshop. National Wildlife Federation, Scientific and Technical Series No. 12.

Haug, E.A., B.A. Millsap, and M.S. Martell. 1993. *The Birds of North America*, No. 61. The Academy of Natural Sciences of Philadelphia, PA.

Hayes, G.E. and J.B. Buchanan. 2001. Draft Washington State Status Report for the Peregrine Falcon. Washington

Department of Fish and Wildlife, Olympia, Washington. 105 pp.

Hayward, G.D. 1989. Habitat use and population biology of Boreal Owls in the northern Rocky Mountains, USA. Ph.D. Dissertation. University of Idaho, Moscow.

Hayward, G.D. 1994. Review of technical knowledge: Boreal Owls. Pages 92-127 in: (G.D. Hayward and J. Verner, eds.) Flammulated, Boreal, and Great Grey Owls in the United States: A technical conservation assessment. USDA Forest Service, Rocky Mountain Forest and Range Experiment Station, Gen. Tech. Rep. RM-253.

Hayward, G.D. and R.E. Escano. 1989. Goshawk nest-site characteristics in western Montana and northern Idaho. Condor 91:476-479.

Hayward, G.D. and J. Verner, eds. 1994. Flammulated, Boreal, and Great Grey Owls in the United States: a technical conservation assessment. USDA, Forest Service General Technical Report. RM-253, 211 pp.

Hayward, G.D., P.H. Hayward, and E.O. Garton. 1993. Ecology of the Boreal Owl in the northern Rocky Mountains. Wildlife Monographs 124:1-59.

Hegdal, P.L. and R.W. Blaskiewicz. 1984. Evaluation of the potential hazard to Barn Owls of talon (brodifacoum bait) used to control rats and house mice. Environ. Toxicol. Chem. 3:167-119.

Hennessey, S.P. 1978. Ecological relation ships of accipiters in northern Utah - with special emphasis on the effects of human disturbance. M.S. Thesis, Utah State University, Logan 66 pp.

Henny, C.J. and R.G. Anthony. 1989. Bald Eagle and Osprey. Pages 66-82 in: Proc. western raptor management symposium and workshop. National Wildlife Federation, Washington, D.C.

Henny, C.J. and J.E. Cornely. 1985. Recent Red-shouldered Hawk range expansion into Oregon including first specimen record. Murrelet 66:29-31.

Henny, C.J. and M.W. Nelson. 1981. Decline and present status of breeding Peregrine Falcons in Oregon. Murrelet 62:43-53.

Henny, C.J. and J.L. Kaiser. 1996. Osprey population increase along the Willamette River, Oregon, and the role of utility structures, 1976-1993. Chapter 12. Pages 97-108 in: (D.M. Bird, D.E. Varland, and J.J. Negro, eds.) Raptors in human landscapes. Academic Press, Ltd. London. 396 pp.

Henny, C. J., L. J. Blus, and T. E. Kaiser. 1984. Heptachlor seed treatment contaminates hawks, owls, and eagles of Columbia Basin, Oregon. Raptor Reseach 18: 41-48.

Henny, C.J., R. A. Olsen, and T.L. Fleming. 1985. Breeding chronology, molt, and measurements of Accipiter Hawks in northeastern Oregon. Journal of Field Ornithology 56:97-112.

Henry, M.E. 1983. Home range and territoriality in breeding White-tailed Kites. Master's thesis, San Diego State Univ., San Diego, CA.

Herron, G. B., C. A. Mortimore, and M. S. Rawlings. 1985. Nevada Raptors: their biology and management. Nevada Department of Wildlife, Reno, Nevada. 114 pp.

Hershey, K.T., E.C. Meslow, F.L. Ramsey. 1998. Characteristics of forests at Spotted Owl nest sites in the Pacific Northwest. Journal of Wildlife Management 62:138-1410.

Herter, D.R. and L.L. Hicks. 2000. Barred Owl and Spotted Owl populations and habitat in the central Cascade Range of Washington. J. Raptor Research 34:279-286.

Hickey, J.J. 1969. Peregrine Falcon Populations: their biology and decline. University of Wisconsin Press, Madison, WI. 596 pp.

Hickey, J.J., and D.W. Anderson. 1968. Chlorinated hydrocarbons and eggshell changes in raptorial and fish-eating birds. Science 162:271-273.

Hickey, J.J., and D.W. Anderson. 1969. The Peregrine Falcon: life history and population literature. Pages 3-44 in: Hickey, J.J. 1969. *Peregrine Falcon Populations: Their Biology and Decline.* University of Wisconsin Press, Madison, WI.

Hodson, K.A. 1976. The ecology of Richardson's Merlins on the Canadian prairies. M.S. Thesis, Univ. of British Columbia, Vancouver, BC.

Hoffman, S.W., W.R. DeRagon, and J.C. Bednarz. 1992. Patterns and recent trends in counts of migrant hawks in western Northern America. HawkWatch International, Salt Lake City, UT.

Holt, D.W. and S.M. Leasure. 1993. Short-eared Owl. *The Birds of North America*, No. 62. The Academy of Natural Sciences of Philadelphia, PA.

Holthuijzen, A.M.A., W.G. Eastland, A.R. Ansell,, M.N. Kochert, R.D. Williams, and L.S. Young. 1990. Effects of blasting on behavior and productivity of Prairie Falcons. *Wildlife Society Bulletin* 18:270-281.

Hooper, T.D. and M. Nyhof. 1986. Food habits of the Long-eared Owl in south-central British Columbia. *Murrelet* 67:28-30.

Houston, C. S., D. G. Smith and C. Rohner. 1998. Great Horned Owl (*Bubo virginianus*). *The Birds of North America*, No. 372. The Academy of Natural Sciences, Philadelphia, PA. 27 pp.

Houston, C.S. and F. Scott. 1992. The effect of man-made platforms on Osprey production at Loon Lake, Saskatchewan. *Journal of Raptor Research* 26 :152-158.

Howie, R. R., and R. Ritcey. 1987. Distribution, habitat selection, and densities of Flammulated Owls in British Columbia. Pages 249-254, In: Symposium, biology and conservation of northern forest owls. USDA Forest Service General Technical Report RM-142. 319 pp.

Hunt, G.W. 1988. The natural regulation of Peregrine Falcon populations. Pages 667-676 in: (Cade, T.J., J.H. Enderson, C.G. Thelander and C.M. White, eds.) Peregrine Falcon Populations: their management and recovery. The Peregrine Fund Inc., Boise, ID.

I

Irwin, L.L., D.F. Rock, and G. P. Miller. 2000. Stand structures used by Northern Spotted Owls in Managed Forests. J. *Raptor Res.* 34:175-186.

Isaacs, F.B., R.G. Anthony, M. Vander Heyden, C. Miller, and W. Weatherford. 1996. Habits of Bald Eagles wintering along the Upper John Day River, Oregon. *Northwest Science* 70:1-9.

Iverson, G.C., G.D. Hayward, K. Titus, E. DeGayner, R.E. Lowell, D. Coleman Crocker-Bedford, P.F. Schempf, and J. Lindell. 1996. Conservation assessment for the Northern Goshawk in southeast Alaska. USDA Gen. Tech. Report, PNW-GTR-387, Portland, OR.

J

Jackson, J. A., I. D. Prather, R. N. Conner, and S. P. Gaby. 1978. Fishing behavior of Black and Turkey Vultures. *Wilson Bull.* 90: 141-143.

James, D. A., and J. C. Neal. 1986. *Arkansas Birds: Their Distribution and abundance.* University of Arkansas Press. Fayetteville, Arkansas.

Janes, S.W. 1984. Influences of territory composition and interspecific competition on Red-tailed Hawk reproductive success. *Ecology* 65:862-870.

Janes, S.W. 1985. Habitat selection in raptorial birds. Pages 159-190 in: *Habitat Selection in Birds* (ed. M.L. Cody). Academic Press, Inc., Orlando, FL.

Janes, S.W. 1987. Status and decline of Swainson's Hawks in southeast Oregon: the role of habitat and interspecific competition. *Oregon Birds* 13:165-179.

Janes, S.W. 1994. Partial loss of Red-tailed

Hawk territories to Swainson's Hawks: relations to habitat. *Condor* 96:52-57.

Jewett, S. A., W. A. Taylor, W. T. Shaw, and J. W. Aldrich. 1953. *Birds of Washington State*. University of Washington Press. Seattle, Washington. 767 pp.

Johnsgard, P.A. 1988. *North American Owls: Biology and Natural History*. Smithsonian Institution Press, Washington, DC. 295 pp.

Johnsgard, P.A. 1990. *Hawks, Eagles, and Falcons of North America*. Smithsonian Institution Press, Washington, DC. 403 pp.

Johnson, D.H. 1993. Spotted Owls, Great Horned Owls, and forest fragmentation in the Central Oregon Cascades. MS Thesis, Oregon State Univ., Corvallis. 125 pp.

Johnson, D.R. and W.E. Melquist. 1973. Unique, rare and endangered raptorial birds of northern Idaho: nesting success and management recommendations. Univ. of Idaho - USDA Forest Service, No. R1-73-021.

Johnson, R.R., L.T. Haight, and J.M. Simpson. 1979. Owl populations and species status in the southwestern states. Pages 40-59 in: (P. Schaeffer and S. Ehlers, eds.) *Owls of the West: Their Ecology and Conservation*. National Audubon Society, Western Education Center, Tiburon, CA.

Jones, S. 1979. Habitat management series for unique or endangered species. Report No. 17. The *Accipiters* — Goshawk, Cooper's Hawk, Sharp-shinned Hawk. USDI BLM Technical Note T/N 335, DSC, Federal Center Building 50, Denver, CO.

Joy, S.M., Reynolds, R.T., and D.G. Leslie. 1994. Northern Goshawk broadcast surveys: hawk response variables and survey costs. *Studies in Avian Biology* 16: 24-30.

K

Kahl, J.R. 1971. Osprey habitat management plan. Lassen National Forest, US Forest Service. No. 2620.

Kehoe, M. 1982. Nesting Hawk-Owls in Lake of the Woods County. *Loon* 54:182-185.

Keister, G.P., Jr. and R.G. Anthony. 1983. Characteristics of Bald Eagle communal roosts in the Klamath Basin, Oregon and California. *Journal of Wildlife Management* 47:1072-1079.

Keister, G.P., Jr., R.G. Anthony and E.J. O'Neill. 1987. Use of communal roosts and foraging areas by Bald Eagles wintering in the Klamath Basin. *Journal of Wildlife Management* 51:415-420.

Kennedy, A. J., F. J. VanThienen, and R. M. McKelvey. 1982. Winter foods of Snowy Owls on the southern coast of British Columbia. Vancouver Natural History Society Discovery 11: 119-121.

Kennedy, P.L. and D.W. Stahlecker. 1993. Responsiveness of nesting Northern Goshawks to taped broadcasts of 3 conspecific calls. *Journal of Wildlife Management* 57: 249-257.

Kirk, D. A., and M. J. Mossman. 1998. Turkey Vulture (*Cathartes aura*). The *Birds of North America*. No. 339. The Academy of Natural Sciences, Philadelphia, PA. pp 31.

Knight, R.L. and R.E. Jackman. 1984. Food-niche relationships between Great Horned Owls and Common Barn-Owls in eastern Washington. *Auk* 101:175-179.

Knight, R.L. and D.G. Smith. 1982. Summer raptor populations of a Washington Coulee. *Northwest Science* 56:303-309.

Knight, R.L. and S.A. Temple. 1986. Methodological problems in the study of avian nest defence. *Animal Behaviour* 34:561-566.

Knight, R.L., D.G. Smith, and A. Erickson. 1982. Nesting raptors along the Columbia River in north-central Washington. *Murrelet* 63: 2-8.

Knight, R.L., D.E. Andersen, M.J. Bechard, and N.V. Marr. 1989. Geographic variation in nest-defence behaviour of the Red-tailed Hawk. Ibis 131:22-26.

Knight, R.L., P.J. Randolph, G.T. Allen,

L.S. Young and R.J. Wigen. 1990. Diets of nesting Bald Eagles, *Haliaeetus leucocephalus*, in western Washington. *Canadian Field-Naturalist* 104:545-551.

Knopf, F. L. 1994. Avian assemblages on altered grasslands. Pages 247-257 in: (J. R. Jehl, Jr., and N. K. Johnson, eds.) A century of avifaunal change in western North America. *Studies in Avian Biology* No. 15.

Kochert, M.N. 1986. Raptors. Pages 313-349 in: (Cooperider, A.Y., R.J. Boyd, H.R. Stewart, eds.) Inventory and Monitoring Wildlife Habitat, US Dept. Interior, BLM, Serv. Ctr., Denver, CO, 858 pp.

L

Larrison, E.J. 1977. A sighting of the Broad-winged Hawk in Washington. *Murrelet* 58:18.

Laymon, S.A. 1991. Diurnal foraging by Spotted Owls. *Wilson Bulletin* 103:138-140.

Leary, A. W. 1996. Home ranges, core use areas, and dietary habits of Ferruginous Hawks in south-central Washington. M.S. Thesis, Boise State University, Boise, Idaho. 72 pp.

Leder, J.E. and M.L. Walters. 1980. Nesting observations for the Barred Owl in western Washington. *Murrelet* 60:110-112.

Lein, M.R. and G.A. Weber. 1979. Habitat selection by wintering Snowy Owls (*Nyctea scandiaca*). *Canad. Field-Nat.* 93:176-178.

Lehmkuhl, J.F. and M.G. Raphael. 1993. Habitat pattern around Northern Spotted Owl locations on the Olympic Peninsula, Washington. *Journal of Wildlife Management* 57:302-315.

Lilieholm, R.J., W.B. Kessler and K. Merrill. 1993. Stand density index applied to timber and goshawk habitat objectives in Douglas-Fir. *Environmental Management* 17:773-779.

Littlefield, C.D., S.P. Thompson, and R.S. Johnstone. 1992. Rough-legged Hawk habitat selection in relation to livestock grazing on Malheur National Wildlife Refuge, Oregon. *Northwestern Naturalist* 73:80-84.

Littlefield, C.D., S.P. Thompson, and B.D. Ehlers. 1984. History and present status of Swainson's Hawks in southeast Oregon. *Raptor Research* 18: 1-5.

Littlefield, C.D. 1990. *Birds of Malheur National Wildlife Refuge, Oregon.* Oregon State University Press, Corvallis, OR. 294 pp.

M

MacWhirter, R.B. and K.L. Bildstein. 1996. Northern Harrier. *The Birds of North America*, No. 210. The Academy of Natural Sciences of Philadelphia, PA.

Maestrelli, J.R. 1973. Propagation of Barn Owls in captivity. *Auk* 90: 426-428.

Marks, J.S., D.L. Evans, and D.W. Holt. 1994. Long-eared Owl. *The Birds of North America*, No. 133. The Academy of Natural Sciences of Philadelphia, PA.

Marks, J.S., D.P. Hendricks, and V.S. Marks. 1984. Winter food habits of Barred Owls in western Montana. *Murrelet* 65:27-28.

Marshall, D.B. 1992a. *Threatened and sensitive wildlife of Oregon's forests and woodlands of Oregon.* Audubon Society of Portland, OR. 66 pp.

Marshall, D.B. 1992b. *Status of the Northern Goshawk in Oregon and Washington.* Audubon Society of Portland, OR. 34 pp.

Marti, C.D. 1988. The Common Barn Owl, Pages 535-550 in: *Audubon Wildlife Report* 1988/1989 (W. J. Chandler, ed.), Academic Press. San Diego, California

Marti, C.D. 1992. Barn Owl. *The Birds of North America,* No. 1. The Academy of Natural Sciences of Philadelphia, PA.

Marti, C.D. 1997. Lifetime reproductive success in Barn Owls near the limit of the species range. *Auk* 114: 581-592.

Marti, C.D. 1987. Raptor food habits studies. Pages 67-80 in: *Raptor Management Techniques Manual* (Eds. B.A. Pendleton, B.A. Millsap, K.W.

Cline, and D.M. Bird), Vol. 1, National Wildlife Federation, Washington, D.C., Sci. Tech. Series No. 10.

Marti, C.D. and J.S. Marks. 1989. Medium-sized Owls. Pages124-133 in: Proceedings of the Western Raptor Management Symposium and Workshop. National Wildlife Federation, Scientific and Technical Series No. 12.

Martin, J.W. 1987. Behavior and habitat use of breeding Northern Harriers in south western Idaho. *Journal of Raptor Research* 21:57-66.

Martin, J.W. 1989. Harriers and kites. Pages 83-91 in: Proceedings of the Western Raptor Management Symposium and Workshop. National Wildlife Federation (Washington), Scientific and Technical Series No. 12.

Mazur, K.M., S.D. Frith, and P.C. James. 1998. Barred Owl home range size and habitat selection in the boreal forest of central Saskatchewan. *Auk* 115:746-754.

McCallum, D. A. 1994a. Conservation status of Flammulated Owls in the United States. Pages 74-79 in: (Hayward, G.D. and J. Verner, eds.) Flammulated, Boreal, and Great Grey Owls in the United States: a technical conservation assessment. USDA, Forest Service General Technical Report. RM-253.

McCallum, D. A. 1994b. Flammulated Owl (*Otus flammeolus*). *The Birds of North America.* No. 93. The Academy of Natural Sciences. Philadelphia, PA.

Miller, G.S., R.J. Small and C.E. Meslow. 1997. Habitat selection by Spotted Owls during natal dispersal in western Oregon. *Journal of Wildlife Management* 61:140-150.

Mitchell, L.C. and B.A. Millsap. 1990. *Buteos* and Golden Eagles. Pages 50-62 in: Proc. of the Southeast Raptor Management Symposium and Workshop, National Wildlife Federation (Washington, DC) Sci. and Tech. Series No. 14.

Mitchell, W. R., and R. E. Green. 1981. Identification and interpretation of ecosystems of the western Kamloops forest region. Vol. 1. Province of British Columbia, Ministry of Forests. Victoria.

Moore, K.R. and C.J. Henny. 1983. Nest site characteristics of three coexisting *Accipiter* hawks in northeastern Oregon. *Raptor Research* 17:65-76.

Mosher, J.A., M.R. Fuller and M. Kopeny. 1990. Surveying woodland raptors by broadcast of conspecific vocalizations. Journal of Field Ornithology 61:453-461.

N

Newton, I. 1979. *Population Ecology of Raptors.* Buteo Books, Vermillion, South Dakota.

Nelson, B.B. and K. Titus. 1988. Silvicultural practices and raptor habitat associations in the Northeast. Pages 171-180 in: Proceedings of the Northeast Raptor Management Symposium and Workshop, National Wildlife Federation, Washington, DC.

Nero, R.W. 1980. *The Great Grey Owl – Phantom of the Northern Forest.* Smithsonian Institution Press, Washington, DC, USA.

O

Oeming, A.F. 1955. A preliminary study of the Great Grey Owl in Alberta with observations of other owl species. Thesis. University of Alberta, Edmonton, Canada.

Olendorff, R. R. 1993. Status, biology, and management of Ferruginous Hawks: a review. Raptor Research and Technical Assistance Center, Special Report USDI BLM, Boise, Idaho. 84 pp.

Olendorff, R.R., A.D. Miller, and R.N. Lehman. 1981. Suggested practices for protection on power lines: the state of the art in 1981. Raptor Research Report No. 4, Raptor Research Foundation, Inc. 111 p.

P

Pagel, J.E. and D.A. Bell. 1997. Reply to Cade et al. Regarding de-listing the American Peregrine Falcon. *Wildlife Society Bulletin* 25:739-742.

Pagel, J.E., D.A. Bell, and B.E. Norton. 1996. De-listing the American Peregrine Falcon: is it premature? *Wildlife Society Bulletin* 24:429-435.

Palmer, R.S. (Ed.). 1988. *Handbook of North American Birds*. Diurnal Raptors (Part 1). Yale University Press, New Haven, Connecticut.

Parmelee, D. F. 1992. Snowy Owl (*Nyctea scandiaca*). *The Birds of North America*, No. 10. The Academy of Natural Sciences, Philadelphia, PA.

Phipps, K. B. 1979. Hunting methods, habitat use and activity patterns of Prairie Falcons in the Snake River Birds of Prey Natural Area, Idaho. Master's Thesis, Western Illinois University. Macomb, Illinois.

Platt, J.B. 1973. Habitat and time utilization of a pair of nesting Sharp-shinned Hawks (*Accipiter striatus velox*). M.S. Thesis, Brigham Young University, Provo, UT.

Platt, J.B. 1977. The breeding behavior of wild and captive Gyrfalcons in relation to their environment and human disturbance. Ph.D. Diss., Cornell University, Ithaca, NY.

Platt, S.W. and J.H. Enderson. 1989. Falcons. Pages 111-117 in: Proceedings of the Western Raptor Management Symposium and Workshop. National Wildlife Federation, Scientific and Technical Series No. 12.

Powers, L.R. 1996. Wintering Sharp-shinned Hawks (*Accipiter striatus*) in an urban area of southwestern Idaho. *Northwestern Naturalist* 77:9-13.

Price, J., S. Droege, and A. Price. 1995. *The Summer Atlas of North American Birds*. Academic Press. New York and London. 364 pp.

R

Ralph, S.C. 1980. Wintering Bald Eagle census along the mainstream Skagit River, Washington, from Sedro Wooley to Rockport, 1979-80. Pages 147-162 in: (R.L. Knight, G.T. Allen, M.V. Stalmaster and C.W. Serveen, eds.) Proceedings of the Washington Bald Eagle Symposium, The Nature Conservancy, Seattle, WA.

Ratcliffe, D. 1980. *The Peregrine Falcon*. Buteo Books, Vermillion, SD. 416 pp.

Reynolds, R.T. 1970. Nest observations of the Long-eared Owl (*Asio otus*) in Benton County, Oregon, with notes on their food habits. *Murrelet* 51:8-9.

Reynolds, R.T. 1983. Management of western coniferous forest habitat for nesting Accipiter hawks. USDA Forest Service General Technical Report RM-102, Rocky Mountain Forest and Range Experiment Station, Fort Collins, Colorado.

Reynolds, R.T. 1989. *Accipiters*. Pages 92-101 in: Proceedings of the Western Raptor Management Symposium and Workshop. National Wildlife Federation (Washington), Scientific and Technical Series No. 12.

Reynolds, R.T. and B.D. Linkhart. 1984. Methods and materials for capturing and monitoring Flammulated Owls. *Great Basin Naturalist* 44:49-51.

Reynolds, R.T. and E.C. Meslow. 1984. Partitioning of food and niche characteristics of coexisting Accipiter during breeding. *Auk* 101:761-779.

Reynolds, R. T., R. A. Ryder, and B. D. Linkhart. 1989. Small forest owls. Pages 134-143 in: Proceedings of the western raptor management and workshop. National Wildlife Federation Scientific and Technical Series No. 12.

Reynolds, R.T. and H.M. Wight. 1978. Distribution, density, and productivity of *Accipiter* Hawks breeding in Oregon. *Wilson Bulletin* 90:182-196.

Reynolds, R.T., E.C. Meslow, and H.M. Wight. 1982. Nesting habitat of coexisting *Accipiter* in Oregon. *Journal of Wildlife Management* 46:124-138.

Reynolds, R.T., R.T. Graham, M.H. Reiser, R.L. Bassett, P.L. Kennedy, D.A. Boyce, Jr., G. Goodwin, R. Smith, and E.L. Fisher. 1992. Management recommendations for the northern goshawk in the southwestern United

States. USDA Forest Service, Gen. Tech. Report RM-217.

Reynolds, R.T., S.M. Joy, and D.G. Leslie. 1994. Nest productivity, fidelity, and spacing of Northern Goshawks in Arizona. *Studies in Avian Biology* 16:106-113.

Richardson, S.A. 1996. Washington State Recovery Plan for the Ferruginous Hawk. Washington Department of Fish and Wildlife, Olympia, Washington. 63 pp.

Ripple, W.J., D.H. Johnson, K.T. Hershey and E.C. Meslow. 1991. Old-growth and mature forests near Spotted Owl nests in western Oregon. *Journal of Wildlife Management* 55:316-318.

Ripple, W.J., P.D. Lattin, K.T. Hershey, F.W. Wagner, and E.C. Meslow. 1997. Landscape composition and pattern around Northern Spotted Owl nest sites in southwest Oregon. *Journal of Wildlife Management* 61:151-158.

Ritter, L. V. 1983. Growth, development, and behavior of nestling Turkey Vultures in central California. Pages 287-302 in: *Vulture Biology and Management.* (S. R. Wilbur and J. A. Jackson, eds.). University of California Press. Berkeley, California.

Robbins, C.S., B. Bruun, and H.S. Zim. 1983. *Birds of North America.* Golden Press, New York, NY.

Rodrick, E. and R Milner, eds. 1991. Management recommendations for Washington's priority habitats and species. Wildlife Management, Fish Management and Habitat Management Divisions, Wash. Dept. Wildl., Olympia, WA.

Rohner, C. 1997. Non-territorial floaters in Great Horned Owls: space use during a cyclic peak of snowshoe hares. *Animal Behaviour* 53:901-912.

Rohner, C., J.M.N. Smith, J. Stroman, M. Joyce, F.I. Doyle, and R. Boonstra. 1995. Northern Hawk-Owls in the nearctic boreal forest: prey selection and population consequences of multiple prey cycles. *Condor* 97:208-220.

Rosenberg, D.K., C.J. Zabel, B.R. Noon and E.C. Meslow. 1994. Northern Spotted Owls: influence of prey base - a comment. *Ecology* 75:1512-1515.

Rosenberg, K.V. and M.G. Raphael. 1986. Effects of forest fragmentation on vertebrates in Douglas-fir forests. Pages 263-272 in: (Verner, J., M.L. Morrison and C.J. Ralph, eds.) Wildlife 2000: habitat relationships of terrestrial vertebrates. University of Wisconsin Press, Madison, WI.

Rosenfield, R.N., J. Bielefeldt, and R.K. Anderson. 1985. Taped calls as an aid in locating Cooper's Hawk nests. *Wildl. Soc. Bull.* 13:62-63.

Rosenfield, R.N., J. Bielefeldt, and R.K. Anderson. 1988. Effectiveness of broadcast calls for detecting breeding Cooper's Hawks. *Wildlife Society Bulletin* 16:210-212.

Rosenfield, R.N. and J. Bielefeldt. 1993. Cooper's Hawk. *The Birds of North America*, No. 75, The Academy of Natural Sciences of Philadelphia, PA. 23 pp.

Runyan, C.S. 1987. Location and density of nests of the Red-tailed Hawk, *Buteo jamaicensis*, in Richmond, British Columbia. *Canadian Field-Naturalist* 101:415-418.

Rusch, D.H. and P.D. Doerr. 1972. Broad-winged Hawk nesting and food habits. *Auk* 89:139-145.

S

Saunders, L.B. 1982. Essential nesting habitat of the goshawk (*Accipiter gentilis*) on the Shasta-Trinity National Forest, McCloud District. M.S. Thesis, California State Univ., Chico.

Schmutz, J.K., R.W. Fyfe, D.A. Moore, and A.R. Smith. 1984. Artificial nests for Ferruginous and Swainson's Hawks. *Journal of Wildlife Management* 48:1009-1013.

Sealy, S.G. 1967. Notes on the breeding biology of the Marsh Hawk in Alberta and Saskatchewan Blue Jay 25:63-69.

Serrentino, P. 1987. The breeding ecology and behavior of Northern Harriers in Coos County, New Hampshire. MS

Thesis, Univ. Rhode Island, Kingston.

Sharp, B.E. 1992. Neotropical migrants on National Forests in the Pacific Northwest. Prepared for USDA Forest Service by Ecological Perspectives, Portland, OR.

Sharp, D.U. 1989. Range extension of the Barred Owl in western Washington and first breeding record on the Olympic Peninsula. *Journal of Raptor Research* 23: 179-180.

Shuster, W.C. 1980. Northern Goshawk nesting requirements in the Colorado Rockies. *Western Birds* 11:89-96.

Small, A. 1974. *Birds of California*. Winchester Press, New York. 310 pp.

Smith, D.G., and D.H. Ellis. 1989. Snowy Owl. Pages 97-105 in: Proceedings of the Northeast Raptor Management Symposium and Workshop. National Wildlife Federation. Washington, D.C., Scientific and Technical Series No. 13. 353pp.

Smith, D.G. and R.L. Knight. 1981. Winter population trends of raptors in Washington from Christmas Bird Counts. Washington Department of Game, Olympia, WA.

Smith, D.G. and J.R. Murphy. 1973. Breeding ecology of raptors in the eastern Great Basin of Utah. Brigham Young University Science Bulletin, Biological Series 18:1-76.

Smith, D.G., and J.R. Murphy. 1978. Biology of the Ferruginous Hawk in central Utah. *Sociobiology* 3: 79-95.

Smith, D.G. and C.R. Wilson. 1971. Notes on the winter food habits of Screech Owls. *Great Basin Naturalist* 31:83-84.

Smith, D.G., J.R. Murphy, and N.D. Woffinden. 1981. Relationships between jackrabbit abundance and Ferruginous Hawk reproduction. *Condor* 83: 52-56.

Smith, D.G., D. Walsh, and A. Devine. 1987. Censusing Eastern Screech-Owls in southern Connecticut. Pages 255-267 in: Symposium Proceedings Biology and Conservation of northern forest owls. USDA Forest Service General Technical Report RM-142. 319 pp.

Smith, D.G., C.R. Wilson, and H.H. Frost. 1974. History and ecology of a colony of Barn Owls in Utah. *Condor* 76:131-136.

Smith, M.R., P.W. Mattocks, Jr., and K.M. Cassidy. 1997. *Breeding Birds of Washington State*. Volume 4 in: K.M. Cassidy, C.E. Grue, M.R. Smith, and K.M. Dvornich, eds. Washington State GAP analysis - final report. Seattle Audubon Society Publications in Zoology No. 1, Seattle, WA.

Smith, S. A. 1982. Observations of a captive Turkey Vulture attacking live prey. *Murrelet* 63: 68-69.

Speiser, R. 1990. Nest site characteristics of Red-tailed Hawks in western Washington. *Northwestern Naturalist* 71:95-97.

Speiser, R. and T. Bosakowski. 1991. Nesting phenology, site fidelity, and defense behavior of Northern Goshawks in New York and New Jersey. *Journal of Raptor Research* 25:132-135.

Spitzer, P.R. et al. 1978. Productivity of Ospreys in Connecticut-Long Island increases as DDE residues decline. *Science* 202:333-335.

Stalmaster, M.V. 1987. The Bald Eagle. Universe Books, New York, NY. 227 pp.

Stalmaster, M.V. and J.L. Kaiser. 1997a. Winter ecology of Bald Eagles in the Nisqually River Drainage, Washington. *Northwest Science* 71:214-223.

Stalmaster, M.V. and J.L. Kaiser. 1997b. Flushing responses of wintering Bald Eagles to Military Activity. *Journal of Wildlife Management* 61:1307-1313.

Stalmaster, M.V., J.R. Newman, and A.J. Hanson. 1979. Population dynamics of wintering bald eagles on the Nooksack River, Washington. *Northwest Science* 53:126-131.

Steenhof, K. 1998. Prairie Falcon (*Falco mexicanus*). No. 346. *The Birds of North America*. The Academy of Natural Sciences. Philadelphia, PA. 28 pp.

Stinson, D.W. , J.W. Watson, and K.R. McAllister. 2001. Draft Washington State Status Report for the Bald Eagle. Washington Department of Fish and

Wildlife, Olympia, Washington. 90 pp.

Swindle, K.A., W.J. Ripple, E.C. Meslow, and D. Schafer. 1999. Old-forest distribution around Spotted Owl nests in the central Cascades. *Journal of Wildlife Management* 63:1212-1221.

T

Tate, G.R. 1997. Short-eared Owl. Wings over the Americas, The Nature Conservancy, Wings Info Resources/ Species Information and Management Abstracts (www.tnc.org/wings/ wingresource/Seow.html), 15 pp.

Tate, J., and D. J. Tate. 1982. The Blue List for 1982. *American Birds* 36: 126-135.

Taylor, D.M. 1984. Winter food habits of two sympatric owl species. *Murrelet* 65:48-49.

Thomas, J.W. (Ed.). 1979. Wildlife Habitats in Managed Forests: the Blue Mountains of Oregon and Washington. Agriculture Handbook No. 553, U.S.D.A. Forest Service.

Thomas, J.W., E.D. Forsman, J.B. Lint, E.C. Meslow, B.R. Noon, and J. Verner. 1990. A conservation strategy for the Northern Spotted Owl. Interagency Scientific Committee to Address the Conservation of the Northern Spotted Owl, Portland, OR. 427 pp.

Thompson, S.P. and D.K. McDermond. 1985. Summary of recent Northern Harrier nesting in western Washington. *Murrelet* 66:82-84.

Thompson, S. P., R. S. Johnstone, and C. D. Littlefield. 1982. Nesting history of Golden Eagles in Malheur-Harney Lakes Basin, southestern Oregon. *Raptor Research* 16: 116-122.

Thurow, T.L. and C.M. White. 1984. Nesting success and prey selection of Long-eared Owls along a juniper/sage brush ecotone in southcentral Idaho. *Murrelet* 65:10-14.

Tigner, J.R, M.W. Call, and M.N. Kochert. 1996. Effectiveness of artificial nesting structures for Ferruginous Hawks in Wyoming. Chapter 16. Pages 137-144 in: (D.M. Bird, D.E. Varland, and J.J. Negro,

eds.). Raptors in human land scapes. Academic Press, Ltd. London. 396 pp.

Trimble, S.A. 1975. Habitat Management Series for Unique or Endangered Species: Report No. 15 Merlin *Falco columbarius*. USDI Bureau of Land Management Technical Note T-N-271.

Trulio, L.A. 1997. Strategies for protecting Western Burrowing Owls (*Speotyto cunicularia hypugaea*) from human activities. Pages 461-465 in: (Duncan, J.R., D.H. Johnson, and T.H. Nicholls, ed.) Biology and Conservation of Owls of the Northern Hemisphere. USDA Forest Service, Gen. Tech. Report NC-190.

U

U.S. Fish and Wildlife Service. 1982. Pacific Coast recovery plan for the American Peregrine Falcon. U.S. Fish and Wildl. Serv. Unit 1, Denver, CO, 303 pp.

U.S. Fish and Wildlife Service. 1992. Recovery plan for the Northern Spotted Owl - final draft, Volumes 1 and 2. USDI, Fish and Wildlife Service, Portland, OR

U.S. Forest Service. 1988a. Spotted Owl inventory and monitoring handbook. Pacific Northwest Region, USDA Forest Service, Portland, OR, and Pacific Southwest Region, USDA Forest Service, San Francisco, CA 18 pp.

U.S. Forest Service. 1988b. Final supplement to the environmental impact statement for amendment to the Pacific Northwest Regional Guide. Vol. 1. Spotted Owl guidelines. USDA Forest Service, Pacific Northwest Region, Portland, OR. 282 pp.

U.S. Forest Service. 1994. Goshawk monitoring, management, and research in the Pacific Northwest region. USDA Forest Service, 1994 Status Report.

U.S. Forest Service and Bureau of Land Management. 1994. Record of decision for amendments to Forest Service and Bureau of Land Management planning documents within the range of the Northern Spotted Owl. U.S. Government Printing Office, Region 10.

V

Vermeer, K., and K.H. Morgan. 1989. Nesting population, nest sites, and prey remains of Bald Eagles in Barkley Sound, British Columbia. Northwestern *Naturalist* 70:21-26.

W

Waian, L.B. 1973. The behavioral ecology of the North American White-tailed Kite of the Santa Barbara coastal plain. Ph.D. Diss., Univ. of California, Santa Barbara.

Warkentin, I.G. and P.C. James. 1988. Nest-site selection by urban Merlins. *Condor* 90:734-738.

Watson, C., J. Johnson, A. Contreras, T. Crabtree, and J. Gilligan. 1989. *Rare Birds of Oregon*. (O. Schmidt, Ed.) Oregon Field Ornithologists Special Publication No. 5, pp 1-188.

Watson, J.W. 1986. Temporal fluctuations of Rough-legged Hawks during carrion abundance. *Raptor Research* 20: 42-43.

Watson, J.W. 1991. Foraging ecology of Bald Eagles in the Columbia River estuary. *Journal of Wildlife Management* 55:492-499.

Watson, J.W., D.W. Hays, S.P. Finn, and P. Meehan-Martin. 1998. Prey of breeding Northern Goshawks in Washington. *Journal of Raptor Research* 32:297-305.

Watson, J.W. and D.J. Pierce. 1998. Bald Eagle ecology in western Washington with an emphasis on the effects of human activity. Dept. of Fish and Wildlife, Olympia, Washington. 197pp.

Whelton, B.D. 1989. Distribution of the Boreal Owl in eastern Washington and Oregon. *Condor* 91:712-716.

Wheeler, B.K. and W.S. Clark. 1995. *A Photographic Guide to North American Raptors*. Academic Press, San Diego, CA.

White, C.M. 1962. Prairie Falcon displays Accipitrine and Circinine hunting methods. *Condor* 65: 113-115.

White, C.M. and R.W. Nelson. 1991. Hunting range and strategies in a tundra breeding Peregrine and Gyrfalcon observed from a helicopter. *Journal of Raptor Research* 25:49-62.

White, C.M. and T.L. Thurow. 1985. Reproduction of Ferruginous Hawks exposed to controlled disturbance. *Condor* 87:14-22.

Wiggers, E.P. and K.J. Kritz. 1994. Productivity and nesting chronology of the Cooper's Hawk and Sharp-shinned Hawk in Missouri. *Journal of Raptor Research* 28:1-3.

Wiley, J.W. 1975. The nesting and reproductive success of Red-tailed Hawks and Red-shouldered Hawks in Orange County, California. *Condor* 83:132-151.

Wilson, U.W., A. McMillan, and F.C. Dobler. 2000. Nesting, population trend and breeding success of Peregrine Falcons on the Washington Outer Coast, 1980-1998. *J. Raptor Research* 34:67-74.

Witt, J.W. 1990. Productivity and management of Osprey along the Umpqua River, Oregon. *Northwestern Naturalist* 71:14-19.

Z

Zarn, M. 1974. Habitat Management Series for Unique or Endangered Species: Report No. 12 Osprey (*Pandion haliaetus carolinensis*). USDI Bureau of Land Management Technical Note. T-N-254.

Conversion Factors

MULTIPLY THIS	BY	TO CONVERT INTO
Length		
inches (in)	2.54	centimeters
centimeters (cm)	0.3937	inches
feet (ft)	0.3048	meters
meters (m)	3.28083	feet
yards (yd)	0.9144	meters
chains (ch)	66	feet
chains	20.1168	meters
kilometers (km)	1,000	meters
miles (mi)	5,280	feet
miles	1,760	yards
miles	80	chains
miles	1609.3	meters
kilometers	0.62137	miles
miles	1.60934	kilometers
Area		
Acres (ac)	43,560	square feet
Square feet (ft²)	0.0929	square meters
Hectares (ha)	10,000	square meters
Hectares	2.47104	acres
Acres	0.40468	hectares
Acres	0.0015625	square miles
Square miles (mi²)	640	acres
Hectares	0.01	square kilometers
Square miles	2.59	square kilometers
Square kilometers (km²)	100	hectares
Township	36	square miles
Basal Area		
Square feet/ac (ft²/ac)	0.2296	square meters/ha
Square meters/ha (m²/ha)	4.356	square feet/ac

Glossary

A

accipiter: the Genus for a group of woodland hawks with short-wings and long tails.

active Nest: a nest containing eggs or young.

B

BBS: Breeding Bird Survey.

biomass: in food habits studies, the total number of individuals of a particular species times their average body weight.

boreal: northern biogeographical regions below the subarctic zone.

brancher: a young raptor that is still unfledged, but can climb out of the nest under its own power onto surrounding branches or neighboring trees.

brood: the collective group of nestlings raised in a single nest.

buffer: a riparian buffer is the area of vegetation left intact along a stream, lake, or pond during and after timber harvest; and a disturbance buffer is a predetermined radius around a nest or roost site where any kind of disturbance or habitat alteration is prohibited.

buteo: the Genus for a group of large, broad-winged soaring hawks.

C

call: a simple avian vocalization, most raptors lack elaborate songs.

canopy: a layer of foliage in a forest stand. This most often refers to the uppermost layer of foliage, but it can be used to describe lower layers in a multistoried stand.

canopy closure: the degree to which the canopy blocks sunlight or obscures the sky. It can only be accurately determined from measurements taken under the canopy with a densiometer or ocular sighting tube.

carrion: flesh obtained from a carcass of a dead animal.

CBC: Christmas Bird Count, a continent-wide bird count conducted by thousands of volunteer birders which occurs during a two-week period overlapping the Christmas Holiday.

clutch: the entire set of eggs produced in a single nest from one female.

coniferous: evergreen trees that are cone-bearing with needles for foliage.

conspecific: a response to the same species.

crepuscular: active at the twilight hours, dawn and dusk.

cross-fostering: parents rearing young birds of another species, mostly an artificial technique to reestablish young birds into the wild, but sometimes occurs naturally.

D

deciduous: trees that lose their leaves during winter, also known as broadleafs.

dimorphism: difference in color, size, or structure between males and females of the same species.

dispersal: movements of young birds after fledging (juvenile dispersal) or by adults after breeding (postbreeding dispersal).

disturbance: a force that causes significant change in structure and/or composition through natural events such as fire, flood, wind, or earthquake, mortality caused by insect or disease out-breaks, or by human-caused events, e.g., timber harvesting, mining, or cultivation.

diurnal: active during daylight hours.

E

edge: the place where plant communities or successional stages meet, most evident where forest adjoins an opening of some sort.

endangered: a species that is declining and is in danger of extinction throughout a significant portion of their range.

endangered Species Act: A federal law aimed at halting the decline and extinction of wildlife (animal and plant species).

endemic: a species that is unique to a specific locality; having a geographically limited range and/or habitat requirements.

eyrie: nest of a falcon, generally a cliff nest.

extinct: a species which has been completely eliminated, no living individuals.

extirpated: a species that has been eliminated within a specific geographical area, but exists elsewhere within its range.

F

falconiforms: diurnal raptors including hawks, falcons, eagles, kites, harriers, and ospreys.

fledge: the act of leaving the nest by a juvenile raptor under the power of flight.

fledgling: a juvenile raptor that has left the nest under its own power, but is still dependent on its parents for food while it continues to learn hunting skills.

forb: a broad-leaved herbaceous plant (non-grasslike).

forest types: a classification of forestland based on stand characteristics that separate one stand from adjacent stands.

forestland: land that is now, or is capable of becoming, at least 10 percent stocked with forest trees and that has not been developed for nontimber use.

fragmentation: the process of reducing size and connectivity of stands that compose a forest.

H

habitat: the topographical, vegetational, and physical characteristics of a specific environment where a raptor occurs.

hacking: a process of allowing captive-bred raptors more freedom, usually to reintroduce them into the wild.

heterospecific: a response to a different species.

home range: the total area used by a raptor (but not necessarily defended) over a defined time period such as daily, breeding, wintering, or annual.

hovering: a form of flapping flight used by hunting raptors to remain stationary over an area where prey has been spotted.

I

immature: a young bird during the period between juvenile dispersal and first breeding. May retain immature plumage for nearly a year (SY; second-year bird) or several years (ASY; after second-year bird) through first breeding.

interspecific: among two members of different species (heterospecific).

intraspecific: among two members of the same species (conspecific).

incubation period: the period from egg laying to hatching.

irruption: periodic, often irregular, migratory incursions during fall or winter.

J

juvenile: a young non-breeding bird exhibiting all or part of its first (juvenile) plumage of nondowny feathers, called HY (hatching year) or AHY (after hatching year) by banders.

K

kettle: an aggregation of soaring migrant hawks swirling on a rising thermal (mostly observed in the Broad-winged Hawk).

L

lagomorph: rabbits, hares, and pikas.

M

managed forest: any forestland that is treated with silvicultural practices and/or harvested. Generally applied to forestland that is harvested on a scheduled rotational basis.

mature: forest age roughly between 70 and 180 years old. Stand age, diameter of dominant trees, and stand structure at maturity vary by forest cover types and local site conditions. Mature stands generally contain trees with a smaller average diameter, less age-class variation, and less structural complexity than old-growth stands of the same forest type. Commercially-mature forest, for which the annual net rate of growth has peaked, is considered 45 to 60 years old in westside forests.

melanistic: unusually dark or black plumage.

mobbing: harassment of a raptor by one or more smaller birds, intended to drive-out the raptor.

migrant: a species that regularly migrates on a seasonal basis between breeding and wintering areas.

N

neotropical: tropics of the Americas including: South America, Central America north to Mexico's central Highlands, and the West Indies.

nest site: the actual location of the nest within the surrounding habitat.

nestling: young birds between hatching and fledging phases.

nocturnal: active during the night.

NWR: National Wildlife Refuge.

O

occupied nest: a nest site potentially used by a breeding pair, whether or not eggs are laid.

old-growth: Old forests at least 180 to 220 years of age, including "ancient" forests and "virgin" forests (never been cut). Old-growth characteristics include: (1) multilayered canopy with trees of several age classes, (2) a multispecies canopy, (3) the presence of large living trees, some with broken tops and other indications of old and decaying wood (decadence) and structural deformities (e.g., mistletoe), (4) the presence of large standing dead trees (snags) and heavy accumulations of wood, including large logs on the ground, (5) moderate to high canopy closure, and (6) the presence of species and functional processes that are representative of the potential natural community.

overstory: trees that provide the upper most layer of foliage in a forest with more than one roughly horizontal layer of foliage.

owl circle: a simplified description of the home range area of a Northern Spotted Owl. To assure survival of the Spotted Owl, at least 40 percent of the home range circle must be retained in suitable (nesting, roosting, and foraging) habitat.

P

pellet: an indigestible wad of material that is coughed-up containing fur, bones, skulls, beaks, and feathers.

postfledging period: the period between fledging and complete independence.

Postfledging Family Area (PFA): the area used by juvenile raptors during the post fledging period.

productivity: a measure of reproductive success, the number of fledglings produced per occupied nest (nest attempt).

R

raptor: a bird of prey or predatory bird belonging to the Falconiforms or Strigiforms.

range: an area or region throughout which an organism occurs.

recovery: the point at which the measures provided pursuant to the federal Endangered Species Act are no longer necessary.

refugia: locations and habitats that support populations of organisms that are limited to small fragments of their previous geographic range (i.e., endemic populations).

riparian: a distinct vegetative zone which occurs along watercourses, lakes, and wetlands. In dry country, this may be the only area that can support trees.

roost: a perch or site used for resting at night (hawks) or during the day (owls).

S

sapling: young tree growth about 10 to 25 years, and usually less than 10 cm in diameter, generally little canopy lift is apparent.

sawtimber: commercial forest age class, small sawtimber about 40 to 70 years, large sawtimber—often synonymous with mature forest—about 70 to 180 years old.

second-growth forest: relatively young forest that has developed following a disturbance (e.g., clearcutting, serious fire, or insect attack) of the previous old-growth forest.

seral stage: stage of forest succession after stand replacing event such as fire, clearcutting, or windthrow, sequence of seral stages is shrub, sapling, young forest, submature forest, mature forest, and old-growth forest.

snag: a standing dead tree. May be used as a hunting perch, roost site, or nest site. Nests can be in a cavity created by a woodpecker, a torn-out branch, disease (heart rot), a hollow broken-off top, or in a stick nest placed on branches or a broken top.

species: the major subdivision of a genus or subgenus, regarded as the basic category of biological classification, composed of related individuals that resemble one another, are able to breed among themselves, but are not able to breed with members of another species.

sympatric: where two different species overlap in range, limited resources could cause interspecific competition, thereby reducing fitness (reproduction) for one or both species.

stoop: aerial diving behavior used by Falconiforms to capture prey, attack enemies, ward-off intruders, play, or display.

subadult: a preadult bird in transition between its juvenile and definitive plumages, sometimes referred to as immature plumage.

submature: intermediate-aged forest, about 40 to 90 years old, between young and mature forest.

subnivean: underground or under snow, referring to a burrowing species.

subspecies: a population of a species occupying a particular geographic area, or less commonly, a distinct habitat, capable of interbreeding with other populations of the same species.

T

terrestrial: associated with upland habitats as opposed to aquatic or riparian species.

territory: the part of the home range that is defended against neighboring raptors of its own species (intraspecific) and sometimes other species (interspecific).

territorial: a bird that uses displays, calls, threats, and aggressive actions (agonistic behavior) to define a territory boundary or evict intruders.

threatened: species that are not yet considered endangered, but are at risk of declining if no action is taken to alleviate threats to their survival.

tundra: the treeless portion of northern arctic regions.

U

understory: the trees and other woody species growing under the canopies of larger adjacent trees and other woody growth.

V

vagrant: an individual occurring well outside its normal range, most often during migration.

Y

young Forest: pole forest or pole stage, relatively young forest, approximately 20 to 40 years old or 10 to 30 cm in diameter, generally displays a branch-free lower bole (canopy lift).

APPENDIX C

HABITAT USE OF RAPTORS IN THE PACIFIC NORTHWEST
(adapted from Thomas 1979, N = nesting, F = feeding, 1 = primary > 40%, 2 = secondary < 40%)

SPECIES	N/F	Meadow-grassland	Sagebrush Desert	Other Shrubs	Juniper	Deciduous Forest	Coniferous Forest	Mixed Forest	Alpine Meadow-Balds	Rivers, Creeks, Streams	Lakes, Reservoirs, Ponds	Marshes, Bogs, Swamps	Edges	Snags	Logs	Burrows	Cliffs, Rimrock, Canyons	Talus	Caves
Turkey Vulture	N					1	1	1							1		1		1
	F	1	1	1	1	1	1	1	1	1	1		1				1	1	
Osprey	N					1	1	1	2	1	1	1		1			2		
	F	2	2	2						1	1	1		1					
White-tailed Kite	N					1	2	1		1	1	1	1						
	F	1	2	1		2	2	2		1	1	1	1	1					
Bald Eagle	N					1	1	1		1	1		1	2					
	F	2	2			2	2	2	2	1	1	1	1	1					
Northern Harrier	N	1	2	1								1	1						
	F	1	2	1						2	2	1	1						
Sharp-shinned Hawk	N					2	1	1											
	F					1	1	1	1	1			1		1	1			
Cooper's Hawk	N			1		1	1	1		1									
	F					1	1	1		1	1	1	1		1	1			
Northern Goshawk	N					2	1	1						2					
	F					1	1	1	1	1	2	1		1	1				
Broad-winged Hawk	N					1	2	1											
	F					1	2	1		1	1	1	1	1					
Swainson's Hawk	N	1	1	1	1												1		
	F	1	1	1	1							2		1			1	1	
Red-tailed Hawk	N	2	2	2	2	1	1	1		1	1	1	1	2			1		1
	F	1	1	1	1	1	1	1	1	1	1	1	1	1			1	1	
Red-shouldered Hawk	N					1	1	1		1	1	1	1						
	F					1	1	1	1	1	1	1		1					
Ferruginous Hawk	N	1	1	1	1												1	1	1
	F	1	1	1	1	1	2	2						1			2	1	
Rough-legged Hawk	N																		
	F	1	1	1	1				1				1	1	1				
Golden Eagle	N					2	1	1	1					2			1		1
	F	1	1	1	1	2	2	2	1	1	1	2	2	1			1	1	
American Kestrel	N	1	1	1	1	1	1	1		1	1	1	1	1		2	1	1	1
	F	1	1	1	1	2	2	2		2	2	2	1	1			1	1	
Merlin	N					1	1	1						2					
	F	1			1	2	2	2	1	1	1	1	1	1			1		
Peregrine Falcon	N								1	1	1	1	1	2		2	1	1	1
	F	1	1	1	2	2	2	2	1	1	1	1	1	1			1	1	
Gyrfalcon	N	1							1								1		1
	F	1							1	1				1			1	1	
Prairie Falcon	N	1	1	1						1	1						1		1
	F	1	1	1					1	1	1		2				1	2	1
Barn Owl	N					1	1	1		1	1	1	1	1			1		1
	F	1	1	1						1	1	1	1	1			1	1	

HABITAT USE OF RAPTORS IN THE PACIFIC NORTHWEST CONTINUED

(adapted from Thomas 1979, N = nesting, F = feeding, 1 = primary > 40%, 2 = secondary < 40%)

SPECIES		Meadow-grassland	Sagebrush Desert	Other Shrubs	Juniper	Deciduous Forest	Coniferous Forest	Mixed Forest	Alpine Meadow-Balds	Rivers, Creeks, Streams	Lakes, Reservoirs, Ponds	Marshes, Bogs, Swamps	Edges	Snags	Logs	Burrows	Cliffs, Rimrock, Canyons	Talus	Caves
		VEGETATION COMMUNITIES								RIPARIAN ZONES			SPECIAL AND UNIQUE HABITAT COMPONENTS						
Flammulated Owl	N						1						1	1					
	F						1						1	1					
Western Screech-Owl	N				1	1	1	1		1	1	1	1	1			1		2
	F	1			1	1	1	1		1	1	1	1	1			2	1	
Great Horned Owl	N				1	1	1	1	1	1	1	1	1	1			1		1
	F	1	1	1	1	1	1	1	1	1	1	1	1	1			1	1	
Snowy Owl	N	1							1										
	F	1							1	1	1	1		1					
Northern Hawk Owl	N					2	1	2			1		1	1					
	F	1			1	2	1	2	1		1		1	1					
Northern Pygmy-Owl	N					1	1	1		1	1	1	1	1					
	F	1	1	1	1	1	1	1		1	1	1	1	1				1	
Burrowing Owl	N	1	1	1	1											1			
	F	1	1	1	1					2	2		2	1			2	2	
Spotted Owl	N						1	1		1				1					2
	F						1	1		1				1	2				
Barred Owl	N					1	1	1		1	1	1		1					
	F					1	1	1		1	1	1		1	1				
Great Grey Owl	N						1	1					1	1					
	F	1					1	1					1	1					
Long-eared Owl	N				1	1	1	1		1	1	1	2						
	F	1	1	1	1	1	1	1		1	1	1	1						
Short-eared Owl	N	1								2	2	1	1						
	F	1	1	1						2	2	1	1						
Boreal Owl	N						1	2						1					
	F						1	1	1					1					
Northern Saw-whet Owl	N					1	1	1		1	1	1	1	1					
	F					1	1	1	1	1	1	1	1	1					

About the Authors

THOMAS BOSAKOWSKI received his Ph.D. Degree in Zoology from Rutgers University and worked full-time as a professional wildlife biologist for five years for a consulting firm in the Seattle area. There, he conducted surveys for Northern Goshawks, Golden Eagles, Bald Eagles, Ospreys, Spotted Owls, breeding birds, and amphibians in the Cascade Mountains, Olympic Mountains, and the Cariboo Forest Region of central British Columbia. For his dissertation research, he investigated the community ecology of raptors in the Northeast. Dr. Bosakowski has published over 50 scientific papers on raptors, breeding birds, small mammals, amphibians, and fish and recently published a book entitled: *The Northern Goshawk: Ecology, Behavior, and Management in North America.*

DWIGHT G. SMITH conducted his doctoral research on the breeding raptor community in northwestern Utah. while working with the late Dr. Joseph R. Murphy of Brigham Young University. He has since continued his studies of the ecology of animals—primarily birds of prey—throughout much of North America, Siberia, parts of Africa and South America. Dwight has published several hundred articles on avian ecology and other science topics. This is his 14th book. He is currently professor and chairman of the biology department at Southern Connecticut State University in New Haven, Connecticut, where he has taught botany and zoology, ecology, population ecology, and mammalogy for the past 32 years.